TABLE OF CONTENTS

Copyright © 2007 Binnur Tomay, TurkishCookbook.com

1

APPETIZERS

This is a delicious appetizer that will add some colour to your table. It goes with any kind of food.

ROASTED RED PEPPER CHEESE ROLLS
(Közlenmiş, Peynirli Kırmızı Biber)

1 red bell pepper

Filling:

60 gr soft feta cheese or goat cheese, crumbled
1 fresh green onion, finely chopped
1 tbsp extra virgin olive oil
1/2 tsp oregano
1/2 tsp crushed pepper

Cut off the top of the red pepper. Cut it in half and discard the seeds. Set the oven to broil (grill), and heat it up. Place the red pepper on an oven tray, insides facing down and place in the oven. Roast it for about 15 minutes. Afterwards place it in a paper bag for a few minutes so you can peel the skins off easier. Do so, then cut in strips, about 1 inch wide.

Mix the cheese with olive oil, oregano, crushed pepper and fresh green onion in a small plate. Spread the mixture equally on one end of each of the red pepper strips and roll them. Place on a service plate. Garnish with black olives. Serve as an appetizer or with breakfast.

Serve hummus as an appetizer with small, toasted pide slices.

HUMMUS
(Humus)

1 can chickpeas (540 ml), washed, peeled
3 garlic cloves, smashed with salt
Juice from 1 1/2 lemons
3/4 cup tahini (sesame paste)
2 tsp cumin
100 ml water
Salt for taste

Garnish:

2 tbsp sunflower oil
1 tsp red pepper
1 tbsp pine nuts, lightly roasted

Mix all the ingredients using a food processor until it is smooth. Arrange on a service plate and shape with a fork. Heat the sunflower oil in a small skillet and add the red pepper. When the oil starts bubbling, turn the heat off and pour over the hummus. Sprinkle pine nuts all over.

TURKISH-STYLE ZUCCHINI GRATIN
(Kabak Graten)

3 small zucchini

Filling:

1/4 cup feta cheese, crumbled
1 tbsp fresh dill and parsley mixture, chopped

Topping:

1 tsp butter
2 tbsp flour
100 ml milk, warm

This is served as an appetizer. You can also serve this dish with Pilaf with Tomato as a light lunch.

Peel the zucchini. Cut them in half lengthwise. Make a slit around the seeds with the tip of a small knife. Remove and discard the seeds with a teaspoon. Mix the filling ingredients with a teaspoon and fill in the zucchini equally.

In a small pot, melt the butter, add flour and mix them with a wooden spoon. Slowly add warm milk and stir. If you like, you can whisk it. Cover the zucchini with this topping.

Place parchment paper on your oven tray. Arrange the zucchini on it. Preheat the oven to 190 C (400 F). Cook for about 25 minutes until the tops are golden.

MUHAMMARA

1 tablespoonful red pepper paste, if you can't find it; use 2 roasted red peppers instead - do NOT use roasted red pepper in a jar
3/4 cup walnuts
4-5 tablespoonful breadcrumbs
1/2 cup extra virgin olive oil
3 garlic clove (optional)
1 tbsp red pepper, crushed
1 teaspoonful cumin
1 lemon juice

Serve this vegetarian dish with toasted pide (pita) or toasted bread pieces.

Put the walnut, garlic and breadcrumbs in the food processor and pulse 2 or 3 times. Add the lemon juice, red pepper paste (or roasted red peppers), cumin and crushed red pepper. Close the lid of the mixer. While mixing, pour in the olive oil from the small opening at the top. Make sure not to over-mix, the walnuts should still be left in small pieces.

Roasted Red Pepper

Cut off the tops of the red peppers. Discard the seeds. Cut each pepper in half. Set the oven to broil (grill), and heat it up. Place the red peppers on an oven tray (inside facing down) and place in the oven. Roast them for about 15 minutes. Leave them in a paper or plastic bag for about 10 minutes to peel off the skin easily.

You can serve this with any kind of Kebab.

MAMZANA

1 or 2 eggplants, roasted and chopped
1 red pepper, roasted and diced
1 fresh onion, chopped
1 large tomato, diced or 1 cup cherry tomatoes, in halves
1-2 cubanelle pepper, diced
2-3 tbsp parsley, chopped
Salt
Pepper

Sauce:

1-2 garlic cloves, smashed with salt
1 cup yogurt, room temperature

Garnish:

1 tbsp liquid oil
1 tsp hot red pepper

Place roasted eggplants in a service plate. Arrange roasted red pepper, fresh onion, tomato, cubanelle pepper and parsley on top. Sprinkle some salt and pepper. Add yogurt sauce on top. Heat up the oil in a small skillet and add the red pepper. Pour over the dish when you see it start bubbling.

Roasted Eggplant:

Before putting in the oven, make holes on the eggplant with a fork so that it will soften and cook better. Then place on an oven tray and roast for about 35 minutes on broil. Then peel it, remove any hard seeds and place in 2 cups of water with 1/2 lemon juice to prevent dark colour. Leave it in for about 5 minutes. After draining, cut into small pieces with a knife. Alternatively, you can barbecue it until softened.

Serve with toasted pide slices.

CREAMY YOGURT DIP
(Haydari)

1 cup creamy yogurt
2 garlic cloves, smashed with salt
2 tbsp dill, chopped
Pinch of cayenne pepper
Pinch of crushed red pepper
Salt

Mix all the ingredients and place on a service plate. Pour some extra virgin olive oil on top. Garnish with black olives and raddish.

KISIR

1 cup bulgur wheat, large grain
60 ml olive oil
1 onion, diced
1 tbsp tomato paste
1/2 cup lemon juice
1 tsp salt
2 tbsp cumin

Garnish

3-4 tomatoes, diced
4-5 fresh green onions, diced
1 cup chopped parsley

First put the bulgur in a large bowl and pour two cups of hot water on it (it should stay like this for 5 minutes). Meanwhile in a medium sized pot, place the onion and olive oil. Cook until the onions turn light brown. Add the salt, tomato paste, lemon juice and cumin.

Then wash and drain the bulgur and mix it into the pot with a wooden spoon. Cook for about 10 minutes on medium-low heat. Afterwards, cover the lid and set aside for it to cool down.

When it's cold, add garnish ingredients. Toss and serve.

This recipe goes well with Ayran. Keep refrigerated as Kısır is best served cold.

FAVA

2 cups dry fava beans
1 onion, chopped
1 1/2 tsp sugar
1 tbsp extra virgin olive oil
3 cups water
Salt

Garnish:

Extra virgin olive oil
Lemon juice

The night before you make this recipe, soak the fava beans in water and leave overnight. The following day, peel the beans and discard the peels.

To prepare, place all the main ingredients in a medium-sized pot and cook for about 1.5 hours on medium-low heat. Afterwards, mix in a blender until smooth and put in an inch deep serving bowl. When cold, make cuts in diamond shapes as shown in the picture. Pour some olive oil and lemon juice on top before serving.

If you like, you can add some dill or 2-3 mint leaves before blending fava.

You can serve Stuffed Mushrooms while still hot as an appetizer or with any kind of beef or chicken dish.

STUFFED MUSHROOMS
(Mantar Dolması)

6-8 large mushrooms

Filling:

5-6 cherry tomatoes, cut in small pieces
2 tbsp chopped green peppers
1 garlic clove, minced
1 tbsp extra virgin olive oil
1/2 tsp salt
Pepper for taste

Topping:

1 1/2 tbsp breadcrumbs
4-5 tbsp mozzarella, grated
1 tbsp extra virgin olive oil

Clean mushrooms with a soft brush or wipe with a piece of cloth. Don't wash them as they will retain water. Discard the stalks.

Mix all filling ingredients and fill in the mushrooms equally with a teaspoon. Then mix all the topping ingredients and cover the mushrooms with it. Place them in a greased dish suitable for the oven.

Preheat the oven to 175 C (350 F) and bake for about 15 minutes until the top is golden brown. Don't overbake.

ZUCCHINI WITH WALNUT DIP
(Çerkez Kabak)

2 medium sized zucchini, grated
1 tbsp extra virgin olive oil
2 fresh green onions, finely sliced
1/2 cup yogurt
1/4 cup walnuts, crumbled
1 slice of bread, crumbled (French or Italian style)
1 garlic clove, smashed with salt

Sauce:

1 tbsp extra virgin olive oil
1 tbsp red pepper (paprika)
1/2 tsp Cayenne pepper

Saute the zucchini with 1 tbsp olive oil in a pan until all the water evaporates. Let it cool down. Add the rest of the ingredients and toss. Place on a service plate.

To make the sauce, heat up the olive oil in a small pan, add the red pepper in it and turn the heat off. Pour all over the zucchini and serve with toasted pide slices.

RED LENTIL AND MINT SOUP
(Ezo Gelin Çorbası)

1/2 cup red lentils, washed and drained
1/4 cup fine grain bulgur, washed and drained
1/4 cup rice, washed and drained
2 tbsp olive oil or butter
1 onion, chopped
1 garlic clove, finely chopped
1/4 cup diced tomato, in a can
2 tbsp tomato paste
4 or 5 cups chicken stock
1 tsp paprika
1/2 tsp cayenne pepper (optional)
1 tbsp dry mint
Salt
Pepper

Garnish:

2 tbsp butter
1 tsp dry mint

Before serving this heartwarming soup always taste first as you may need to add more salt.

Saute the onion with olive oil for about 2 minutes, then add garlic and saute until the smell of the garlic comes out. Throw the diced tomatoes in and let them soften for about 10 minutes. Add the rest of the ingredients. Cook on high heat to bring to boil then turn down to simmer. Cook for about half an hour, stirring occasionally. Pour into the blender and pulse 3-4 times. Pour back into the pot. If too thick, add more hot chicken stock or water. Melt the butter in a small pan. When you see the bubbles turn the heat off. Add the dry mint and stir. Pour it into the soup, stir and serve with lemon wedges.

MUSHROOM SOUP
(Mantar Çorbası)

200 gr brown mushrooms, brushed, sliced
1 tbsp butter
1 small onion, finely chopped
2 tbsp flour
1/2 tsp salt, adjusted to your liking
1 pinch black pepper
1 pinch crushed red pepper
2 cups chicken broth, at room temperature
1 Bay leaf
1/4 cup cream, half & half

Saute the onion with butter for a few minutes. Take the pot from the heat, add flour, salt, pepper and crushed pepper. Stir using a wooden spoon until creamy. Slowly add the chicken broth while stirring. Throw in the mushrooms and the Bay leaf. Put back on the stove, stir constantly. When it starts bubbling, turn the heat down to medium-low. Cover with the lid and cook for about 20 minutes. Add the cream and stir. Turn the heat off, take the Bay leaf out and serve while still hot.

If you like sprinkle some croutons on top.

RED LENTIL SOUP
(Kırmızı Mercimek Çorbası)

1 cup red lentils, washed and drained
1 onion, chopped
1 small carrot, chopped
1 1/2 cubes beef bouillon
3 cups water

Garnish:

1 tbsp butter
Red pepper
Cayenne pepper

Place all the main ingredients in a medium-sized pot. Cook for about 20 minutes on medium-low heat. Then mix thoroughly using a blender. If necessary (too thick), add more hot water. Pour into soup bowls using a ladle.

Melt the butter in a small pan and add in the peppers. When it starts bubbling, pour over the soup. Serve Red Lentil Soup while still hot with fresh bread. Add a few drops of lemon juice to taste.

Serve with Bread Slices with Garlic, and Kaşar cheese or Mozzarella cheese.

TOMATO SOUP WITH FLAT GREEN BEANS
(Yeşil Fasulyeli Domates Çorbası)

500 gr tomatoes, peeled, cut in cubes
7-8 flat green beans, washed, cut off the tips, cut in 2 cm long chunks
2 tbsp extra virgin olive oil
1 onion, chopped
1 garlic clove, smashed with salt
1 1/2 cup chicken stock or water
1/2 tsp oregano
1/2 tsp salt
Pepper for taste

Saute the onion with olive oil for 3-4 minutes in a pan. Add all the ingredients except the chicken stock. Stir, cover the lid and cook for about 20 minutes over low heat.

Add the chicken stock and bring to a boil, then turn down the heat to medium-low. Cook another 20 minutes until the flat green beans are fork tender. Sprinkle some chopped parsley on top before serving.

Bread Slices with Garlic and Kaşar Cheese

Slice a baton bread. Spread butter with garlic on top. Arrange Kasar or Mozzarella cheese slices on top and sprinkle some Cayenne pepper. Place the bread slices on the oven tray and set the oven to grill. Place the tray on the second rack from the top. Cook for about 3-4 minutes until the cheese melts and takes a light golden colour.

ROASTED EGGPLANT SALAD WITH WALNUTS

(Cevizli Patlıcan Salatası)

2 large eggplants
1/2 lemon juice
50 ml extra virgin olive oil
1/2 tsp cayenne pepper
Salt
Pepper

Topping:

1/3 cup walnuts, crumbled

This salad goes very well with any kind of barbecue or meat dishes.

Before putting them in the oven, make holes on the eggplants with a fork so that they will soften and roast better. Then place them on an oven tray and roast for about 25 minutes on broil. Alternatively, you can barbecue them until softened. Then peel them, remove any seeds and place in a strainer to drain.

Place the roasted eggplants in an ovenproof dish. Cut into small pieces with a knife. Add the lemon juice, olive oil, cayenne pepper, salt and pepper and toss. Sprinkle the walnuts all over.

Place the dish on the second rack from the top in the oven. Grill for about 4 minutes until walnuts become lightly roasted.

TURKISH STYLE TOMATO DIP

(Acılı Ezme)

3 tomatoes, discard the seeds, very finely chopped
1/2 red or white onion, very finely chopped
1 cup parsley, very finely chopped
2 tbsp extra virgin olive oil
1 tsp pomegranate paste or Granadine syrup
2-3 tbsp lemon juice
1 tsp cayenne pepper, crushed
1 tsp sumac
Salt

Sumac comes from the berries of a wild bush which grows in the Mediterranean. The berries are dried and crushed to form purple-red powder. The flavour is sour and fruity and mostly used with Kebabs, preferred to lemon for sourness.

Crush the onion with sumac and salt with your hands. Mix all the ingredients in a service bowl. Put aside for at least an hour (tastes better this way), then serve with any kind of Kebab.

ARUGULA SALAD
(Roka Salatası)

> 1 bunch Arugula, washed and drained
> 1-2 tomatoes, peeled, cut in bite sizes

Dressing:

> 1-2 garlic cloves, smashed with salt
> 2 tbsp lemon juice
> 50 ml extra virgin olive oil
> 1 tsp crushed red pepper
> Salt
> Pepper

Arugula Salad goes best with any kind of seafood dish.

Break off the Arugula stems. Break off the leaves into smaller pieces with your hands. Place on a service plate. Whisk all the dressing ingredients. Pour all over the Arugula and toss. Add tomatoes on top.

SHEPHERD'S SALAD
(Çoban Salatası)

> 1/2 cup cucumber, diced
> 2 tomatoes, diced
> 1 cubanelle pepper
> 1/2 red onion, sliced
> 1/4 cup fresh mint
> 2 tsp lemon juice
> 2-3 tbsp extra virgin olive oil
> 50 ml feta cheese, crumbled
> Salt
> Pepper

This quite populer salad goes very well with any kind of dish Summer or Winter.

Place all the vegetables in a medium size salad bowl. Add salt and pepper to liking. Add the feta, lemon juice and olive oil. Don't add any other dressings.

CARROT SALAD
(Havuç Salatası)

> 2 large carrots

Sauce:

> 3 tbsp extra virgin olive oil
> 1/2 lemon
> Salt
> Pepper

Peel, wash and grate the carrots. Place in a salad bowl. Pour in the sauce ingredients and mix. Garnish with black olives.

LAMB TANDIR WITH VEGETABLES
(Sebzeli Kuzu Tandır)

2 Lamb Shanks
1 tsp salt
1/2 tsp pepper

2 medium carrots, peeled, washed, cut in chunks
3 medium white potatoes, peeled, washed, cut in chunks
1/2 cup pearl onions, peeled
4-5 garlic cloves, peeled, sliced
1 cup small mushrooms, brushed
2 tablespoonful crushed tomatoes, in a can
1/2 tsp crushed red pepper

Place the lamb shanks in a large cooking pot. Pour water in until they're all covered. Cook on medium-high heat for about 10 minutes. Remove the foam from the surface. Then reduce heat and simmer. Add the salt and pepper. Occasionally turn the shanks over to cook both sides. When about half the water evaporates, add more hot water to cover the shanks again. Cooking time is about 4 hours.

When 45 minutes are left, cover the shanks with hot water and add the carrots. Cover the lid, increase the heat from simmer to a little bit under medium. After 10 minutes add the potatoes and onions, stir, cover the lid. After 10 more minutes add the rest of the ingredients. Cook with the lid covered until all the vegetables are fork tender.

If you like it juicier, you can add a little bit more hot water. When you turn the heat off, sprinkle some oregano and chopped parsley on top, then cover with the lid. Set aside for about 10 minutes before serving.

LAMB TANDIR
(Kuzu Tandır)

3 pieces Lamb Shanks
1 tsp salt
1/2 tsp pepper

Place lamb shanks in a large steel pan. Pour water until they're all covered. Cook on medium-high heat for about 10 minutes. Remove the foam from the surface. Then reduce heat and simmer. Add the salt and pepper. Occasionally turn the shanks over to cook both sides. When about half the water evaporates, add more hot water to cover the shanks again. Cooking time is about 4 hours.

When you enter the last hour, increase the heat to medium. Turn the shanks over a few times to make sure both sides are equally cooked. When all the water evaporates, turn the heat off and sprinkle some oregano on top.

This recipe is one of the most popular and traditional dishes in Turkish cuisine. The name, "Hünkar Beğendi", literally means "The Sultan liked it".

See TurkishCookbook.com for preparation pictures.

SULTAN'S PLEASURE
(Hünkar Beğendi)

Lamb ingredients:

750 gr boneless lamb stew chunks
2 cups water
1 onion, sliced
1 cubanelle pepper, chopped
1 large tomato, seeds removed and diced
1 garlic clove, sliced
1 tbsp crushed tomato
Salt
Pepper

Eggplant ingredients:

1 kg eggplant
3 cups water with juice of 1/2 lemon and 1 tbsp salt
3 tbsp butter
2 tbsp flour
1 cup milk
2 tbsp mozzarella, grated
Salt
Pepper

First cook lamb with 2 cups of water. While cooking, remove the foam from surface as it forms. When there is little water left, add the onion and garlic. Cook for 5 minutes on medium-low heat. Add the cubanelle pepper, tomato, crushed tomato, salt and pepper. Cover the lid, cook for 15 minutes on medium-low heat. Keep an eye on the water during this time, if there's none left, add a bit more.

Heat the oven on broil. Before putting in the oven, make holes on the eggplants with a fork so that it will soften and cook better. Then place on the tray and roast for about 35 minutes, or until the eggplants soften. Then, peel the eggplants with a knife and cut off the tops. Remove any hard and large pulp inside the eggplants. Put the water with lemon juice and salt in a large bowl. Soak the eggplants in it, so that their colour won't be dark later. Drain and squeeze with your palms after a few minutes.

Melt the butter in a large pot, then add flour, salt and pepper. Keep stirring with a wooden spoon until blended well. Put in the eggplants and mash with a fork. Slowly pour in the milk and beat with a small egg beater. Make sure there are no big eggplant pieces left. Pour in the mozzarella and beat again.

Place the mashed eggplants on a service plate with the centre empty as shown here. Put the lamb in the centre. Serve while still warm.

3-4 servings.

BEEF WITH MUSHROOMS
(Etli Mantar)

200 gr beef, cut in cubes
200 gr mushrooms, sliced
1 onion, sliced
2 garlic cloves, sliced
1 tbsp butter
2 tbsp extra virgin olive oil
1 tbsp tomato paste
2 cups water
1 tsp salt
1/2 tsp pepper

Cook the beef in a medium sized pot with 1 cup water on medium-low heat. Add the butter, olive oil, onion, garlic, salt and pepper. Cook for about 10 minutes, stirring occasionally. Add the tomato paste, mushrooms and another cup water. Put the lid on and cook for another half hour on medium-low heat. You may serve with Turkish Pilaf.

Make sure not to wash the mushrooms as they will retain water and lose texture. Instead, wipe off with a damp paper towel.

FLAT BEANS WITH LAMB
(Kuzu Etli Taze Fasulye)

150 gr lamb cubes
1 onion, chopped
500 gr flat beans, washed, cut off the ends, in bite sizes
50 ml olive oil
4 garlic cloves, sliced
2 tbsp crushed tomato, in can
1 cup + 2 cups hot water
Salt
Pepper

Cook the lamb cubes with its own juice. After all the water evaporates, add the onion and olive oil, saute for a few minutes. Add 1 cup of hot water, cook over medium-low heat until all the water evaporates and the lamb pieces soften. Then add rest of the ingredients with 2 cups of hot water. Cover the lid halfway and cook for 35 minutes until the beans become soft (but not too much) over medium heat. If necessary add more hot water.

* If you like to store some fresh Flat Green Beans in the freezer to cook later, first wash them and cut off the ends. Bring to a boil water with salt in the pot. Throw the beans in and boil for 2 minutes and drain. Divide them up and place them in ziploc bags. Keep in the freezer. When you want to cook them, you don't need to defrost.

While you're cooking this, put away 7-8 flat green beans to make Tomato Soup with Flat Green Beans (page 8).

LAMB KAVURMA
(Kuzu Kavurma)

> 1 kg Boneless Lamb Stew Chunks
> 4 cups warm water
> 1 medium sized onion, sliced
> Salt
> Pepper

Garnish:

> 1 tsp oregano

Sprinkle some dry oregano on top and serve with Shepherd's Salad and Pilaf.

In a large pot place lamb and warm water. Cook on medium high to get the water boiling. After 10 minutes, remove the foam from the surface with a wooden spoon.

Then add the onion, salt and pepper. After 15 minutes lower the heat. Simmer until most of the water evaporates. This will take approximately 5 to 6 hours. When the water level is at the top of the meat level, turn the heat up to medium. When the water evaporates, stir constantly for 4-5 minutes to prevent the lamb from sticking. Be careful not to over-cook.

GRAPE LEAF ROLLS
(Yaprak Sarması)

> 1 lb grape leaves, washed one by one

Filling:

> 1 1/4 lb medium or regular ground beef, uncooked
> 1/2 cup rice, washed and drained
> 1/4 cup water
> 50 ml extra virgin olive oil
> 1 onion, finely chopped or grated
> Salt
> Pepper

Garnish:

> 3 tbsp crushed tomatoes
> 60 ml butter, diced

See TurkishCookbook.com for preparation pictures.

Mix all the filling ingredients in a bowl with a tablespoon. Fill a large pot half way with water and boil. Add in all the leaves and boil for about 2-3 minutes. Drain, then cut off the stems. The matte (not shiny) side of the leaf is the inside, that's where the filling will go. Grab a leaf and fold the top where the stem was. Put the leaf into your palm and use a teaspoon to put filling on it.

First fold over the top, then the two sides and roll to close it up. Line up all the rolls in a large pot tightly, without big holes in between. Spread the garnish on top. Put a small plate upside down over the rolls - this is to prevent the rolls from unfolding while being cooked. Then pour in a cup of water. Cook on medium-low heat for 20 minutes. Add 1 1/2 cup of hot water, and cook for another 15 minutes. Let cool for 10 minutes, then serve.

EGGPLANT MOUSSAKA
(Patlıcan Musakka)

Large eggplant
200 gr medium ground beef, cooked
1 onion, sliced
1 or 2 garlic cloves, sliced
1/4 red bell pepper, sliced
1/2 cubanelle pepper, diced
2 fresh green onions, chopped
4 tbsp crushed tomato
Salt
Pepper
1/2 cup sunflower oil

You may serve this traditional Ottoman dish with pilaf.

Peel the eggplant skin in strips lengthwise. Cut the eggplant vertically in 3-4 pieces, each about 1 inch thick. Then cut again horizontally, each piece about 2 inches long. Soak in water with a tablespoon of salt for about 30 minutes. Then dry with paper towels. Pour the sunflower oil in a large skillet. Fry both sides of the eggplants until the colour turns medium brown. After frying, place the eggplants on a plate with paper towel to soak up extra oil.

Meanwhile, cook the ground beef with the onions, tomato, garlic, salt and pepper. Then add the red pepper, cubanelle pepper and fresh green onions and cook for about 5-6 more minutes. Lay out the eggplant pieces in another pan. Put the beef mixture over the eggplants. Pour half a cup of water on top. Cook on medium heat for 15 minutes covered with the lid.

STEAK WITH VEGETABLES AND TOMATO SAUCE
(Salçalı Biftek)

1 piece beef steak
1 tbsp butter
3/4 cup + 1/2 cup hot water mixed with 2-3 tbsp crushed tomato, in can
1 small onion, sliced
1 garlic clove, sliced
1-2 mushrooms, brushed, sliced
4-5 slices of green pepper
4-5 slices of red pepper
1 tsp extra virgin olive oil
Salt
Pepper

Fry the beef steak with butter on both sides for a few minutes over medium heat. Then turn the heat down to medium-low. Add the crushed tomato mixture, onion and garlic, and cook until the water evaporates. Place the rest of the ingredients around the steak with 3/4 cup of hot water and cook for about 5-6 minutes on low heat with the lid on until some of the water evaporates. Serve with the cooked vegetables with juice over the top. Garnish with chopped fresh onions, crushed pepper and oregano.

STUFFED EGGPLANTS WITH GROUND BEEF
(Karnıyarık)

4 small eggplants
1/2 cup sunflower oil
3/4 cup hot water with 1 tbsp crushed tomato

Filling:

150 gr medium ground beef
1 small onion, sliced
1 medium tomato, put aside 4 thin slices, dice the rest
1 small cubanelle pepper, put aside 4 thin slices, chop the rest
1-2 garlic cloves, sliced
Salt
Pepper
1 tbsp crushed tomato
3/4 cup hot water

Serve Karnıyarık while still warm with Pilaf and Ayran.

Peel alternating strips of skin lengthwise as seen in the picture for each eggplant. Sprinkle salt on top and put aside for about 20 minutes. Squeeze, wash and dry them with a paper towel. Heat the oil in a skillet over medium-high heat and fry every side until nicely colored. Cut a slit in each eggplant and scoop out most of the seeds, making sure they don't fall apart. Place them in a clean pan.

Meanwhile cook all the filling ingredients in a small pot on medium heat. All the water should evaporate. Stir constantly towards the end.

Fill the eggplants equally with the filling using a teaspoon. Place the sliced tomato and green pepper on each eggplant. Pour 3/4 cup of hot water with 1 tbsp crushed tomato into the pan from the side. Cover the lid. Cook on medium-low heat for about 15 minutes.

CHICKPEAS WITH GROUND BEEF
(Kıymalı Nohut)

1 can of chickpeas
1 onion, chopped
2 tbsp olive oil
3 tbsp regular or medium ground beef
2 tbsp crushed tomato
1 cup warm water
1 tsp salt
1 tsp cumin
Pepper for taste

Chickpeas with Ground Beef is very easy to make and tastes great, especially when served with Pilaf.

Cook the onion and ground beef in a pot. Then add the rest of the ingredients and continue cooking on medium heat with the lid half-covered for another 10-15 minutes.

STUFFED ZUCCHINI

(Kabak Dolması)

 5 small zucchini, washed
 150 ml hot water
 2 tbsp crushed tomato
 2 tbsp extra virgin olive oil

Filling:

 150 gr medium ground beef
 2 tbsp rice, washed and drained
 3 fresh onion, chopped
 50 ml water
 Salt
 Pepper

Sauce:

 1/2 cup yogurt
 2 tbsp dill, chopped
 1 garlic clove, smashed
 Salt

Wash the zucchini and cut off a thin slice of the bottom of each one, so that they can stand up straight. Cut off the tops (as in the picture) and carve out the insides. Mix all the filling ingredients with a teaspoon and stuff the zucchini. Leave some room at the top. While filling the zucchini, don't push the filling in, instead tap the zucchini vertically on the counter. Place them in a small cooking pot.

Mix the hot water, crushed tomato and olive oil and pour into the pot from the side. Cover the lid and cook for about 20 minutes over medium heat.

Place cooked zucchini on a service plate. Pour some of the sauce from the pot on top of them. Mix the yogurt sauce ingredients and do the same.

BEEF STEW WITH ONIONS

(Soğanlı Yahni)

 250 gr beef, cubed
 1 pkg (~300 gr) pearl onions, peeled
 A few slices of orange peel
 2 tbsp butter
 50 ml extra virgin olive oil
 2 tbsp tomato, crushed
 Salt
 Pepper

Cook the beef first in a medium sized pot with 1 1/2 cups of water on medium-low heat. Check to make sure the beef is done through. Then add in the rest of the ingredients along with another 1 1/2 cups of water.

Cook for about 35 minutes on medium-low heat.

Sprinkle some oregano and chopped parsley and serve.

POTATO MOUSSAKA
(Patates Musakka)

6 medium sized white potatoes, peeled and sliced 3/4 inches thick
150 gr medium or regular ground beef, cooked
1 onion, sliced
1 garlic clove, sliced
3 tbsp crushed tomato (or 1 large tomato)
1 tbsp butter
4 tbsp extra virgin olive oil
2 cups water
1/2 tsp crushed pepper (optional)
Salt
Pepper

Garnish:

1/4 cup parsley, chopped

This is a very easy recipe. Place the potatoes in a large, deep skillet. Then add all the ingredients in the above order on top. Cook for about 20 minutes on medium-low heat. Wait for 10 minutes before serving.

Place Çaput Aşı on a service plate, put a few spoons yogurt with garlic on top and serve.

LAMB WITH GRAPE LEAVES
(Çaput Aşı)

250 gr grape leaves, fresh or in jar
250 gr lamb cubes, cooked with water
1 large onion, sliced
1/3 cup rice, washed and drained
3 tbsp butter
3 tbsp crushed tomato in a can

Sauce:

1 garlic clove smashed with salt
1/2 cup yogurt

Soak the leaves in hot water for 2-3 minutes, then drain. Cut off the stems. Cut the leaves in chunks and place in a pot. Throw the cooked lamb and sliced onions on it. Now add the rice, crushed tomato, butter, 1 cup hot water, salt and pepper. Cook on medium-low heat with the lid covered. Check the water occasionally and if necessary, slowly add more hot water, until the rice is done.

EGGPLANT KEBAB

(Pathcan Kebap)

2 Chinese or Japanese eggplants, washed, cut in 3 cm thick pieces
3-4 cubanelle peppers, washed
2-3 medium tomatoes washed, cut in halves
4-5 garlic cloves, unpeeled

Meatball Ingredients:

300 gr medium ground beef
Salt
Pepper

Garnish:

Extra virgin olive oil
Mozzarella, grated
Crushed red pepper
Salt
Pepper

Knead the meatball ingredients. Shape them into medium sized balls. While maintaining the order of the eggplant pieces, alternate meatball and eggplants while skewering.

Preheat your barbecue or oven (grill). Place the skewers on the rack along with the peppers, tomato halves (inside up) and garlic cloves. Make sure to turn the skewers so that all sides of the meat and eggplants are cooked equally.

How to Serve Eggplant Kebab

Cut the meatballs into small pieces with a knife on a plate. Peel the eggplants and garlic cloves. Also peel the peppers, discard the seeds and cut in small pieces. Peel the tomatoes, cut in small pieces. Add olive oil, red pepper, salt and black pepper on top of everything and toss them. Finally sprinkle some grated cheese on top. Wrap it with pide (pita) or arrange into a pocket pita.

CHESTNUT KEBAB

(Kestane Kebap)

When buying chestnuts, choose the fat ones, as they will be more delicious when grilled. Soak the chestnuts in water for about 15-20 minutes to get them to soften. Using a small knife, cut the shells horizontally on the top (fat) side. Turn the oven on to broil. Place the chestnuts in an oven tray and put it on the middle rack. Turn them over after 15 minutes and roast for another 10 minutes. Take them out and let them cool for about 10 minutes. Eat while still warm after removing the shells.

ISKENDER KEBAB

(İskender Kebap)

2 pieces of beef tenderloin, each 200 gr
200 gr regular ground beef
4 pieces of Asian Nan Pita bread or plain pita bread (pide)
Salt
Pepper

Garnish:

Yogurt
1 cup tomato paste, heated up with a few tbs of water
(or use canned crushed tomatoes)
2 tbsp butter

Add the salt and pepper to the ground beef. Knead and give it a round shape, then place in the middle of the two pieces of tenderloin.

Cover in plastic wrap and leave in the freezer overnight. The next day remove from the fridge 45 minutes before cutting. Use a knife, electric knife or meat cutter to shred it. Then fry in a large pan (be careful not to over-fry).

Cut the pitas in bite size diagonal shapes and place on the plates. Spread the beef over the pita bread pieces. Pour the tomato sauce on top and place a few spoons of yogurt on the side. Lastly, melt the butter in a small pan. When it starts bubbling, pour over the tomato sauce. Serve Iskender Kebab while still hot.

SHRIMP KEBAB

(Karides Kebabı)

Large Shrimp, as much as you want, frozen or fresh, peeled and de-veined
1 red bell pepper, cut in chunks, equal amount as shrimp
Medium mushrooms, equal amount as shrimp, brushed
1 or 2 lemons, cut in 8s, equal amount as shrimp

Marinade:

50 ml extra virgin olive oil
2-3 tbsp lemon juice
2-3 garlic cloves, smashed with salt
Red pepper, crushed, optional
Salt
Pepper

If you use wood skewers, dip them in water first.

Arrange lemon, shrimp, red pepper and mushrooms on the skewers. In a bowl, whisk the marinade ingredients. Brush the marinade all over the ingredients on the skewers. Leave them in the fridge for one hour.

Preheat your barbecue or oven (grill/broil). Place the skewers on the rack and cook for about 3-4 minutes. Flip the other side and cook another 2-3 minutes.

ALİ NAZİK

2 medium eggplants or roasted eggplant in a jar
1 large cubanelle pepper or regular green pepper
150 gr medium or regular ground beef, cooked with salt and pepper
1/2 cup yogurt with salt and smashed garlic, at room temperature

Garnish:

1 tbsp butter
1 tsp red pepper, powdered
1/2 tsp Cayenne pepper, powdered

Ali Nazik originates from the Gaziantep Region of Turkey.

Set the oven to broil (grill), and heat it up. Make holes in the eggplants with a fork so that it will roast better. Place the eggplants and green pepper on an oven tray and place in the oven. Roast the green pepper for about 15 minutes and the eggplant for about 35-40 minutes. Turn them over occasionally during roasting.

Peel off the skins from both the eggplant and green pepper (discard seeds), and cut in small pieces. Put them in a pyrex dish (I used 10 inch / 25 cm round pyrex). Put back in the warm oven. Note that at this point the oven's turned off, and you just want to keep the food warm.

Also if you used roasted eggplant in a jar, you should just roast the green pepper. When the rest of the ingredients are prepared, take the pyrex out of the oven and pour the yogurt on top. Then put the cooked ground beef on top of the yogurt. Lastly, melt the butter in a small pan and add the peppers. When it starts bubbling, pour over the ground beef. Serve while still warm.

CHICKEN SHISH KEBAB

(Tavuk Şiş Kebap)

350 gr chicken breast, boneless, cut in medium sized cubes
2 large tomatoes, cut in halves
2 cubanelle pepper

Marinade:

1/2 cup plain yogurt
1/2 tsp cumin
1 tsp red pepper, powder
1/2 tsp cayenne pepper
1 garlic clove, smashed with salt
1 tsp pomegranate paste
2 tbsp olive oil

Marinate the chicken overnight in the fridge in a container with a lid. Bring the chicken to room temperature one hour before grilling. Divide up the chicken cubes and place on four skewers.

Preheat the barbecue or oven (grill). Place the skewers on the rack along with the peppers, tomato halves (inside up). Keep the marinade aside. Grill the chicken for about 7-8 minutes. Make sure to turn the skewers so that all sides are cooked equally. Every time you turn the chicken, brush with marinade.

Serve with roasted Cubanelle peppers and tomato halves.

SIMIT KEBAB

(Simit Kebabı)

Kofte Ingredients:

250 gr medium ground beef
1/3 cup bulgur, small grain
1 onion, grounded
2 garlic cloves, smashed with salt
1 tsp crushed red pepper
1 tsp cumin
2 tbsp pine nuts
1 cup parsley, chopped
1 tsp salt
Pepper for taste

2-3 cubanelle pepper
2-3 tomatoes, halved

Garnish:

Mozzarella (Kaşar cheese), grounded
Pistachio, grounded

Soak the bulgur in hot water for 10 minutes to get it softened. Drain and wash. Add the rest of the kofte ingredients and knead well. Leave it in the fridge for an hour. Make walnut sized balls. Arrange the meatballs on the skewers.

Preheat the barbecue or oven (grill). Place the skewers along with the peppers and tomato halves (inside up) on the grill tray. Place the tray on the second rack from the top of the oven. Make sure to turn the skewers so that all sides of the meatballs are cooked equally. Leave it in for about 20 minutes.

Place the pide (pita) on the service plates. Cut them in bite size. Arrange the Kebabs on the pides. Sprinkle grated Mozzarella (Kaşar cheese) and pistachio over the tops of the Kebabs.

DONER KEBAB

(Pilav Üstü Döner)

2 pieces of beef tenderloin, each 200 gr
200 gr medium ground beef
Salt
Pepper

Add the salt and pepper to the ground beef. Knead and give it a round shape, then place in the middle of the two pieces of tenderloin. Cover in plastic wrap and leave in the freezer overnight.

The next day remove from the fridge 45 minutes before cutting. Use a knife, electric knife or meat cutter to shred it. Then fry the slices in a large pan.

TURKISH STYLE PIZZA WITH GROUND BEEF
(Lahmacun)

1 package Original Tortillas (Flat Bread, 10 pieces)
500 gr lean ground beef
2 medium onions
1 cup parsley
1 tbsp red pepper paste
2 large tomatoes, seeds discarded
1 tsp flaked peppers
1 garlic clove
1 tsp salt

Serve with parsley with red onion slices and Ayran while they're still warm.

Use a mixer to chop and mix all the ingredients except the ground beef. Then knead it with the ground beef. Refrigerate for an hour, then leave it outside for 20 minutes. Set the oven to grill (broil). Have two oven trays ready. Take some mixture with the spatula and apply on the flat bread evenly as a thin layer. Place two per oven tray and put the trays on the second rack from the top in the oven. Bake for about 3-4 minutes, making sure not to burn the edges of the pitas. Place a paper towel at the bottom of a large pot. Fold the cooked Lahmacun in half and put them in the pot to keep them warm with the lid closed.

TURKISH SHISH KEBAB
(Şiş Kebap)

500 gr lamb, cut in medium sized cubes

Marinade:

50 ml milk
3 tbsp extra virgin olive oil
1 small onion, grated
Salt
Pepper
3 tomatoes, cut in half
3 cubanelle peppers, cut in half, seeds discarded
1 onion, peeled, cut in 8s

Pour all the marinade ingredients all over the lamb cubes and toss. Cover it with plastic wrap and allow it to marinate overnight in the fridge. The following day let it sit at room temperature for 1 hour before cooking.

Arrange lamb cubes on the skewers. Make 2 skewers for 1 serving. Preheat the barbecue or oven (grill). Place the skewers on the rack along with the peppers, tomato halves and onion. Make sure to turn the skewers so that all sides of the lamb are cooked equally for a total 10 minutes.

CHICKEN & SEAFOOD

You can serve this simple and delicious Turkish recipe to your guests by adding Patty Shells.

CHICKEN WITH POTATOES
(Patatesli Tavuk)

4 pieces of chicken, dark and white
5 medium white potatoes
2 tbsp crushed tomatoes
1 onion, sliced
4 garlic cloves, sliced
1/2 cubanelle pepper, chopped
1/2 red pepper, chopped
1 fresh green onion, chopped
60 ml olive oil
1/2 tsp crushed pepper
Salt
Pepper

For presentation:
2 Patty Shells (Tenderflake), frozen

Place the chicken in a large pot and cover with 2 cups of water. Cook for about 20 minutes over medium-low heat. Remove the foam from the surface with a spoon. Then add all the other ingredients. Cook all together approximately for 20-25 minutes until the potatoes are fork tender. If necessary add a little more hot water.

Meanwhile bake the Patty Shells following the instructions on the box. Place them on the service plate. Remove the tops with a fork and fill the shells with some potatoes and serve them together.

CHICKEN WITH CABBAGE
(Kapuska)

1/2 head of cabbage, cut in medium sized chunks
4 pieces of chicken, dark or white
3 tbsp rice, washed and drained
1 red bell pepper, discard the seeds, cut in medium sized chunks
2 tbsp butter
3 tbsp extra virgin olive oil
1 tsp red pepper paste
2 tbsp crushed tomato, in a can
1 tsp red pepper, crushed
1/2 lemon juice
Salt
Pepper
1 or 1 1/2 cup hot water

Place the cabbage in a large pot. Add the chicken pieces in along with the rest of the ingredients. Cover the lid and cook for about half an hour over medium heat. Check the water towards the end to see if it is necessary to add more. Don't put too much water in the beginning, the cabbage will leave water during cooking.

CHICKEN IN WHITE SAUCE

(Fırında Meyaneli Tavuk)

1 whole chicken
1 medium onion, chopped
1 garlic clove, chopped
2 fresh green onions, chopped
1 zucchini, cut in medium sized chunks
1 tsp salt
Pepper

Sauce:

3 tbsp extra virgin olive oil
1/4 cup flour
1 cup warm milk

Garnish:

1 cup Kasar cheese (or Mozzarella), shredded
11 x 7 x 1.5 in 2 L Pyrex dish

Boil the whole chicken with water in a large pot (add one peeled whole onion in it, discard after boiling). Take the chicken out of the stock* and let it cool down. Then remove one piece of chicken breast**. Usually a whole chicken is too much for the sauce. Discard the skin and all the bones from the remaining chicken.

Tear it apart in medium sized chunks with your fingers. In a large skillet, cook the onion with 2 tbsp olive oil on medium-low heat for a few minutes. Then add the garlic, salt and pepper. Saute until the smell of the garlic comes out.

Add the flour, stir and slowly pour the warm milk*** in it while stirring constantly. The milk and flour should blend very well. You can use an egg beater. Turn the heat off. Mix the chicken, zucchini and green onions with the flour sauce and arrange them in the Pyrex dish. Sprinkle the shredded cheese on top.

Preheat the oven to 200 C (400F) and bake for about 40-45 minutes until the colour of the top turns golden.

* Cook Chicken Soup with Rice with the chicken stock.
** Also try cooking Okra with Chicken with the leftover chicken breast the next day.
*** If you use cold milk, the sauce may curdle.

OKRA WITH CHICKEN
(Tavuklu Bamya)

1 chicken breast, cooked in water and cut in chunks
375 gr (drained weight) okra, in a can, washed and drained
2 tbsp chickpeas, in a can
8-10 cherry tomatoes, cut in half
50 ml extra virgin olive oil (half for cooking, rest for after)
1/2 cup hot water
1 tsp salt

Sauce:

Juice 1 lemon
1 garlic, smashed
1 tsp dry mint

Place all the ingredients in a medium pot. Cover the lid and cook for about 20 minutes on medium-low heat. Add the second half of the olive oil when finished. Mix the sauce ingredients and pour all over. Mix them carefully so that the okra don't get smashed.

Serve Shrimp Gratin as an entree with a spoon because all the juice will come out - it is very delicious.

SHRIMP GRATIN
(Karides Güveçte)

175 gr shrimp, cooked, de-veined and peeled
1 large tomato, peeled, cut in small cubes
1/2 cubanelle pepper, cut in small pieces
2 fresh green onions, chopped, white parts only
1 garlic clove, chopped
2 tbsp cream
1 tsp butter
Salt
Pepper

Topping:

1 tsp butter
2 tbsp flour
100 ml milk, warm
1/4 cup Kasar or Mozzarella cheese, grated

Mix all the ingredients in a small bowl. Divide into 2 individual ovenproof bowls. Put aside.

To make the topping melt the butter in a small pot. Add the flour, stir and slowly pour the warm milk* in it while stirring constantly. The milk and flour should blend very well. You can use an egg beater. Turn the heat off. Toss the grated cheese in it. Cover the shrimp with this topping in the bowls.

Place the bowls on the oven tray. Preheat to 400 F (200 C). Cook until the tops take a golden colour.

* If you use cold milk, the sauce may curdle.

TIGER SHRIMP SALAD WITH FLAT GREEN BEANS

(Yeşil Fasulyeli Karides Salatası)

250 gr tiger shrimp, cooked, deveined and peeled
4 tomatoes, peeled and diced
1/4 red onion, sliced
2 green onions, chopped
250 gr flat green beans, boiled in salted water and cut in bite sizes
2 tbsp parsley, chopped

Sauce:

1/4 cup mayo
2 tbsp cream
1 tbsp lemon juice
1/2 tsp crushed pepper (optional)
1 tsp salt
1/2 tsp pepper

Whisk the sauce ingredients. Then mix all the salad ingredients in a large bowl. Pour the sauce all over and toss. Place on a service plate. You can serve this dish at room temperature or after chilling it in the fridge.

HALIBUT STEAK WITH TOMATO SAUCE

(Domates Soslu Kalkan Balığı)

Sprinkle some chopped parsley and lemon juice on top before serving.

2 Halibut steaks (Kalkan is a large Turkish flatfish,
    though not available in North America)
1 tbsp extra virgin olive oil
1 tsp butter
1 onion, sliced in rings
2 tomatoes, peeled, discard the seeds, diced
1 tbsp crushed tomato in can + 1/2 cup hot water
4 mushrooms, brushed, sliced
1 tbsp cream
Salt
Pepper

Sautee the onion with butter and olive oil for about 4-5 minutes. Add water with crushed tomato, salt, pepper and halibut steak. Cover the lid. Cook for about 10 minutes over medium-low heat. Turn them over halfway. Add the mushrooms around the halibut and cook for another 2-3 minutes. Then add the cream and stir. Turn the heat off.

Place the Halibut steaks on a service plate. Pour the sauce with mushrooms all over.

Garnish with lemon slices and parsley before serving.

HADDOCK FILLETS WITH SAUCE
(Soslu Mezgit Balığı)

250-300 gr Haddock (or Sole etc.) fillets, 4 pieces frozen
1 tbsp butter
1 onion, copped
1 garlic clove, chopped
125 gr mushrooms, sliced
1 medium tomato, peeled and diced
1 tbsp crushed tomato, canned
Salt
Freshly ground black pepper
3/4 cup water
125 gr shrimp, frozen or fresh, cooked, peeled and deveined

Sauce:

1 egg yolk
1/4 cup cream
2 tbsp lemon juice

Garnish:

4 lemon slices
2 tbsp parsley, finely chopped

Sautee the onion with butter for 3-4 minutes in a pan. Add the garlic and when the smell comes out, add the mushrooms, tomato, crushed tomato, salt, pepper and stir. Place 4 fillets on top of the vegetables in the pan. Add the water. First turn the heat to high. When the water starts bubbling, turn the heat down and simmer. Cover the lid and cook for 10 minutes. Place the fillets on a service plate. Cover with aluminum foil to keep them warm.

Add the shrimps into the pan, cook until half of the remaining water evaporates. Meanwhile, whisk the egg yolk, lemon juice and cream. Pour slowly into the pan. Mix and turn the heat off. Don't boil the cream mixture. Pour all over the fish.

FISH SALAD
(Balık Salatası)

~250-300 gr Sole Fillets, Bluefish, etc
1 tbsp extra virgin olive oil

Sauce:

8 tbsp mayonnaise
1 tbsp Dijon mustard
1 tbsp lemon juice
1 tbsp dill, chopped
1 tsp red pepper, crushed
Salt
Pepper

Cook both sides of the Sole Fillets equally with 1 tbsp olive oil in a pan. Don't overcook as it easily gets dry. Then cut them in chunk sizes. Place on a service plate. Let it cool down. Mix all the sauce ingredients and cover the fish with the sauce.

TURKISH NOODLES WITH MIXED VEGETABLES

(Sebzeli Erişte)

Medium size noodles for two people
1 small eggplant, peeled and cut in small pieces
   (soak in salted water for 20 min.)
1 small zucchini, peeled and cut in small cubes
7-8 cherry tomatoes, cut in half
2 garlic cloves, sliced
1 medium onion, sliced
2 tbsp, 1 tbsp extra virgin olive oil
3 tbsp crushed tomatoes, in can
1/2 cup hot water
1 tsp red pepper paste
1 tsp salt
Pepper for taste

You can also use rice instead of noodles if you prefer.

Sautee the onion with olive oil in a medium pan. Add the garlic. When it starts to smell, add all the other ingredients. Cover the lid and cook on medium-low heat for about 20-25 minutes. In the meantime, boil the noodles. Drain, put 1 tbsp olive oil all over and stir. Place the noodles in two service plates. Put the cooked vegetables on top.

PASTA WITH YOGURT SAUCE

(Yoğurtlu Makarna)

2 servings of bowtie pasta
1 1/2 tbsp butter
Salt

Sauce:

1/2 cup yogurt, room temperature
2 garlic cloves, smashed with salt

Boil the pasta with salted water following the instructions on the package, drain. Melt the butter in a pot. Toss the pasta and add salt. Place pasta on a service plate. Mix all the sauce ingredients and pour all over.

This is one of the easiest and most delicious rustic Turkish dishes. Serve with Turkish Bread, tomato and cucumber slices.

TURKISH NOODLES WITH ARUGULA
(Rokalı Erişte)

2 cups large egg noodles
1 bunch Arugula, washed, drained, torn up with your hands
2 tbsp butter or extra virgin olive oil
Salt
Pepper

Garnish:

Walnuts, crumbled

You may serve this traditional Ottoman dish with rice.

Boil the egg noodles and drain. Melt some butter (or olive oil) in a cooking pot. Add the noodles, salt and pepper and cook for a few minutes on low heat. Toss arugula over it.

Arrange the noodles on a service plate, sprinkle walnuts all over. Serve with yogurt.

See Turkish Cookbook.com on how to make Turkish Noodles (Erişte).

PASTA IN THE OVEN
(Fırında Makarna)

250 gr penne pasta

Sauce:

4 tbsp butter
1/4 cup flour
1 cup milk, warm
4 eggs
1/2 tsp nutmeg
Salt
Pepper
2/3 cup feta cheese, crumbled
1/4 cup parsley, chopped

Garnish:

2/3 cup kasar or mozzarella cheese, grated

2L Pyrex dish, oiled

Boil the pasta with salted water following the instructions on the package, drain. Place in oiled Pyrex dish.

Meanwhile prepare the sauce. Melt the butter, add the flour, stir and cook about 3-4 minutes in a medium-sized pot. Slowly pour in the warm milk while stirring constantly. The milk and flour should blend very well. Add the nutmeg, salt and pepper. Turn the heat off. Let it cool down for 3-4 minutes. Then add the eggs one by one, mix very well. Add feta cheese and parsley to one half of the sauce, toss it with the pasta in the Pyrex dish. Then add the Kasar or Mozzarella cheese into the rest of the sauce. Cover the pasta with it equally.

Preheat the oven to 400 F and bake for about 30 minutes until the top takes a golden colour.

TURKISH RICE PILAF

(Pilav)

> *3/4 cup long-grain rice*
> *1 cup hot water or chicken stock*
> *2 tbsp butter*
> *1 tsp salt*
> *Pinch pepper*

Wash the rice several times with warm water and drain. Then cover the rice with hot water and leave for about 15 minutes, then drain. Melt the butter in a cooking pot. Saute the rice with butter for 2-3 minutes while stirring. Pour 1 cup of hot water or chicken stock in it. Add salt and pepper. Turn the heat to low and cook until the rice absorbs all the water.

Take the cooking pot away from the heat. Open the lid, place a clean kitchen towel across the top of the pot on the rim and put the lid on it. Let the Pilaf stand for about 5 minutes. We call this brewing time. Then serve.

* Don't stir Pilaf while it's cooking.
* Don't use a spoon to fluff Pilaf. Use a wooden or regular fork for it.

You can serve Turkish Rice Pilaf with any kind of meal. My favourite is having this delicious pilaf with plain yogurt and some chopped fresh green onions (only white parts) all over.

PILAF WITH ALMONDS

(Bademli Pilav)

> *1 cup rice, washed and drained*
> *2 cups water*
> *1 tbsp butter*
> *1/2 cup bleached almonds*
> *1 tsp salt*

Roast the almonds in a medium-sized pot until they're light brown. Put aside.

Pour the water in a medium sized pot along with salt and butter. When it starts boiling, add the rice. Cook on low heat with the lid half covered until the water has evaporated. Then add roasted almonds and stir. Serve while still warm.

PILAF WITH LAMB
(Etli Pilav)

> 2 lamb shanks
> 1 cup rice
> 4-5 fresh green onions, cut into little pieces
> 2 medium size tomatoes, diced
> Salt, pepper
> 30 ml. butter, diced

First, place lamb shanks in a medium sized pot. Cover with water and cook on medium-high for 35-40 minutes. When finished, separate the meat, discard the bones, strain and put aside the remaining stock for use later.

Place washed, uncooked rice in a large skillet (not a pot). Put the lamb pieces between the rice equally. Put tomatoes, green onions, butter, salt and pepper as well around the lamb. Then, take the stock from before and pour it over. The stock should be 1 3/4 cups, if not, you can add water. Keep the lid half covered and cook on medium-low heat for approximately 20-25 minutes until the rice is cooked (water should be completely absorbed).

Serve warm or cold with Yogurt on the side. It is a great dish, especially for lunch.

BULGUR PILAF WITH SPINACH
(Ispanaklı Bulgur Pilavı)

> 1 cup bulgur, large grain, washed and drained
> Half bunch of spinach, roots cut off, washed and drained
> 1 medium size onion, cut in small pieces
> 3 tbsp extra virgin olive oil
> 1 tbsp red pepper paste
> 1 3/4 cup hot water
> 1 tsp crushed red pepper
> 1 tsp cumin
> Salt
> Pepper

Saute the onion with olive oil for a few minutes. Add all the ingredients except the spinach and stir. Cook it over low heat with the lid on. When you start seeing holes on the surface of the bulgur add the spinach and stir slowly. Cook for about 5 more minutes.

SULTAN'S PILAF
(Sultan Pilavı)

1 medium eggplant, peeled, cut in bite sizes
1 large tomato, peeled, discard the seeds, cut in cubes
1/4 cup bleached almonds, slivered

Plain pilaf:

1 cup rice
2 cups hot water
2 tbsp butter
Salt
Pepper

Mini meatballs:

150 gr ground beef
1 egg
1 tbsp breadcrumbs
Salt
Pepper

For Frying:

1 tbsp flour
1/2 cup sunflower oil

Garnish:

Some dry oregano

First cook the rice, cover the lid and put aside.

Soak the eggplants in water with salt for 10 minutes to prevent bitterness and darkening of their colour. Squeeze the eggplants with your hands and dry them with a paper towel. Dip them in flour and fry in the sunflower oil until they are evenly colored, but not burnt. Leave them on a paper towel to soak the extra oil. Put aside.

Put the almonds in a pot and toast them for a few minutes. Add the diced tomatoes and cook for about 5 minutes on medium-low heat. Put aside.

Knead the meatball ingredients: ground beef, egg, breadcrumbs, salt and pepper. Make them into balls the size of hazelnuts. Roll them in flour and fry them in the sunflower oil. Take them out with a perforated spoon and place on a paper towel. Sprinkle some oregano on top and put aside.

Add the tomato sauce with almonds and fried eggplants into the pilaf. Mix well and place on a service plate with a hole in the centre. Put the fried meatballs in there and serve while still warm.

OLIVE OIL DISHES & VEGETABLES

Serve Stuffed Peppers cold with fresh lemon juice, after your main dish.

STUFFED PEPPERS WITH OLIVE OIL
(Zeytinyağlı Biber Dolması)

> 5 medium sized peppers
> 2 1/4 cups water
> 1 cup rice, washed and drained
> 4-5 medium sized onions, chopped
> 2 tbsp currants
> 2 tbsp pine nuts
> 1 1/2 tbsp mint
> 1/2 cup extra virgin olive oil
> 4 tbsp sugar
> 1 tsp salt

Sautee the onions with the oil for about 10 minutes in a medium-sized pot. Then add the rice, sugar and salt, stir and cover the lid. Cook on very low heat until the rice looks see through. Add the nuts, currants, mint and a cup of water. Stir occasionally on low heat. Cook until all the water evaporates and put aside.

Cut off the tops of the peppers using a small knife, but don't throw them away as you will put them back on after you stuff the peppers. Discard the seeds inside the peppers.

Stuff the peppers with the filling using a tablespoon. Place the tops of the peppers as seen in the picture above. Put in a medium sized pot along with 1 1/4 cup of water poured over the peppers. Cover the lid, cook until most of the water evaporates on medium-low heat.

FLAT BEANS WITH OLIVE OIL
(Zeytinyağlı Yeşil Fasulye)

> 500 gr flat beans
> 50 ml extra virgin olive oil
> 1 small onion, chopped
> 1 garlic clove, chopped
> 1 tbsp sugar
> 2 tomatoes, diced
> 1 tbsp crushed tomato
> 1 1/2 cups water
> Salt

First, wash the beans, trim both ends and shave along the sides with a knife. In a large pot place the onion and olive oil. Cook them together for about 3-4 minutes. Add the beans, garlic, salt, sugar, tomatoes and crushed tomato. Pour in 1 cup of water. Leave the lid half open and cook for 35-40 minutes, and add another half cup of water midway through. If needed, you can add more water later.

Let cool for half an hour, then place in a service plate. Pour in a little bit of extra virgin olive oil again. Let cool in the fridge. This dish is served cold as a side.

LEEK WITH OLIVE OIL

(Zeytinyağlı Pırasa)

1 bunch of leeks, washed and cut, in chunks
1 medium sized carrot, washed and chopped, bite size
75 ml extra virgin olive oil (half for cooking, half for after)
2 tbsp rice, washed
Juice from half a lemon
1 cup water
1 tbsp sugar
Salt

Place all the ingredients except half of the olive oil in a medium-sized pot. If needed, you can add more water. Cover the lid halfway and cook for about 30 minutes on medium-low heat. After cooking, put on a service plate and pour the remaining olive oil over top. Let cool for a while, then refrigerate. Pırasa is served cold or at room temperature.

CELERY ROOT WITH OLIVE OIL

(Zeytinyağlı Kereviz)

3 small celery roots, or 1 large celery root
1 1/2 cups water
1/2 lemon juice
50 ml extra virgin olive oil
Juice from half an orange
1 tsp sugar
1 tsp salt

Filling:

1 cup carrot, sweet peas and potato mix in a can or frozen

Garnish:

1 tbsp fresh dill, chopped

Sprinkle dill on top and serve when it is cold.

Pour the water and lemon juice in a large bowl. Peel the celery roots. Slice them about 1.5 inches thick (see picture). Hollow out one side with a knife which will be filled with the vegatables. Wash them with water and soak in the lemon juice mixture to prevent them from getting dark.

Place the celery roots in a large pot with the hollow sides facing up. Add the lemon mixture, olive oil, salt, sugar and orange juice on top. Put the lid on and when the water gets hot, cook for about 15 minutes on medium heat.

Add the vegetable mixture in the pot and cook for another 8-10 minutes on medium-low heat. Place them on a service plate. Put the vegetables on each one equally using a spoon.

EGGPLANT WITH VEGGIE FILLING
(İmam Bayıldı)

4 small eggplants
3/4 cup sunflower oil or olive oil

Filling:

1 medium onion, sliced
1 medium tomato, diced
4 garlic cloves, sliced
1 tbsp extra virgin olive oil
1 tbsp sugar
Salt

Garnish:

1 tbsp fresh parsley, chopped

This dish is one of the most well-known olive oil dishes in Turkish Cuisine and it's very tasty.

For each eggplant, peel alternating strips of skin lengthwise as seen in the picture. Sprinkle salt on top and put aside for about 20 minutes. Squeeze, wash and dry them with a paper towel. Heat the oil in a skillet over medium-high heat and fry every side until nicely colored. Cut a slit in each eggplant and scoop out most of the seeds, making sure they don't fall apart. Place them in a clean pan.

Meanwhile cook all the filling ingredients in a small pot on medium heat for about 12-13 minutes. All the water should evaporate. Stir constantly towards the end.

Fill the eggplants equally with the filling using a teaspoon. Pour in 1/2 cup of water in the pan from the side. Cover the lid. Cook on medium heat until almost all the water evaporates. Let cool first, then place on a service plate. Garnish with parsley.

FAVA WITH OLIVE OIL
(Zeytinyağlı Bakla)

400 gr fava bean
2 cups water with 2 tbsp lemon juice
1 small onion, chopped
75 ml extra virgin olive oil (half for cooking, half for after)
2 tbsp sugar
1 tbsp flour
1/4 cup fresh dill, chopped (half for cooking, half for garnish)
Salt

This dish is eaten with yogurt with garlic. Fava bean is available in the summertime only.

Wash the fava. Trim both ends and shave along the sides with a knife. Place in the water with lemon juice so that the colour of the fava won't be dark later.

Sautee the onions with half of the olive oil in a medium-sized pot. Put the fava, 1 cup of lemon water and the remaining ingredients above in the pot. If needed, add the second cup of lemon water. Cook for about 20-25 minutes on medium-low heat with the lid half covered. Place on a service plate and pour the remaining olive oil on top and garnish with the remaining fresh dill. Let cool before putting in the fridge.

BLACK-EYED PEAS
(Börülce)

1 cup black-eyed peas
50 ml extra virgin olive oil
2 tbsp tomato paste
1 cup hot water
1 tbsp sugar
1 tsp salt

Boil the black-eyed peas in 3-4 cups of water until softened (about 20 minutes). Then wash and drain them. Put them in a medium-sized pot with the rest of the ingredients. Cook for about 20-25 minutes on medium heat. Give it a taste towards the end and add more sugar or hot water if necessary. Serve while hot with fresh bread.

GREEN PEPPER & POTATO DISH
(Biber Aşı)

1 medium onion, chopped
1 green pepper, in chunks (don't discard the seeds)
2 medium tomatos, diced
3 medium white potatos, in chunks
3 tbsp rice, washed and drained
50 ml extra virgin olive oil
1 tbsp butter
2 cups warm water
1 tsp salt
Pepper for taste

Sautee the onions with the butter and olive oil in a large pot on medium heat. Add the green peppers with the seeds along with the tomatoes, potatoes, salt and pepper. Cook for about 5 minutes, stirring constantly. Add the water and rice. Cover the lid halfway and cook for about 20-25 minutes on medium heat.

GREEN LENTIL DISH
(Yeşil Mercimek Yemeği)

3/4 cup lentils, soak in water overnight, washed and drained
1 onion, finely chopped
50 ml extra virgin olive oil
1 tsp cumin
3 tbsp crushed tomatoes, in can
1 tbsp orzo, optional
2 cups warm chicken stock or beef stock or just water

Saute the onion with olive oil for about 3-4 minutes. Add the lentils and saute for another 4-5 minutes. Then add the rest of the ingredients. Cook for about 20-25 minutes over medium-low heat until the lentils soften, stir occasionally.

Serve Spinach with Rice with the yogurt sauce.

SPINACH WITH RICE
(Pirinçli Ispanak)

> 1 bunch spinach, washed and drained
> 2 tbsp rice, washed and drained
> 1 garlic clove, sliced
> 1 medium onion, sliced
> 1 medium tomato, diced
> 50 ml extra virgin olive oil
> 1 pinch red pepper
> 1 cup hot water
> Salt
> Pepper

Sauce:

> 1/2 cup yogurt
> 1 garlic clove, smashed
> Salt

First cut the spinach in large pieces. Sautee the onion with olive oil in a medium pot, then add the garlic. Cook for a few minutes until the smell comes out. Be careful not to burn the garlic. Then add the spinach, tomato, rice, red pepper, salt and black pepper in the pot. Cook for a few minutes, stir and add hot water when the spinach soften.

Cover the lid halfway and for cook about 20 minutes (until the rice is cooked) on medium-low heat.

Dible goes very well with chicken and beef dishes as a side. This recipe originates from Northern Turkey, the Black Sea region.

DİBLE

> 500 gr flat green beans, washed, ends cut off and sides trimmed, cut
> 1.5 inches long
> 1 medium sized onion, chopped
> 1/2 cup rice, washed and drained
> 1/2 cup water
> 50 ml extra virgin olive oil
> 1 tsp salt
> 1/2 tsp black pepper

Sautee the onion with olive oil in a pot for about 2-3 minutes. Add the beans, salt and pepper, and cook on medium-low heat for another 5 minutes.

Using a wooden spoon, place the beans in a circle around the edge of the pot. Put the rice in the hole in the middle. Now cover the rice with the beans. Pour the water in from the sides. Cover the lid and simmer for about 30 minutes. Make sure not to open the lid too often to ensure that the heat stays in the pot. Wait until the water evaporates. You can also let it cook a bit longer until the rice is caramelized.

You can serve Dible warm or cold.

BOREK
(Börek)

454 gr (1 lb) Phyllo Pastry
50 ml extra virgin olive oil
2/3 cup milk
1/2 cup water
2 eggs
1 tsp salt
3L (13x9x2") pyrex casserole dish

For this recipe, choose one of the following fillings:

Spinach Filling:

1 pkg (300 gr) frozen chopped spinach
1/4 cup crumbled feta
1 onion, chopped
1 tbsp extra virgin olive oil
Salt
Black pepper

Beef Filling:

250 gr medium ground beef
1 onion, sliced
2 tomatoes, diced
1 small cubanelle pepper, chopped
Salt
Black pepper

This recipe goes well with Cherry Compote on the side or Ayran. You can have it as a main dish or with afternoon tea as a snack.

See TurkishCookbook.com for preparation pictures.

For Spinach Filling: Put the salt, pepper, olive oil and onion in a pan. Cook on medium heat for two minutes. Add the spinach and continue cooking until all liquid has evaporated. Put aside and add the feta cheese.

For Beef Filling: Put the salt, black pepper, ground beef and onion in a pan. Cook on medium heat until the beef is done. Add the tomatoes and the pepper. Continue cooking for another 5 minutes. Put aside.

Now we can move on to the main ingredients. In a bowl, mix the eggs, olive oil, milk and water with a whisk. This liquid mix will go between every two layers of the pastry, and will complement your choice of filling. The spinach or beef filling will go in the middle only.

Grease the casserole dish. Place two sheets of the pastry in the bottom and over the sides of the dish. Spread 2-3 tablespoons of the liquid mix on top. Take another two sheets of pastry, fold in half, and stack in the dish. Continue layering until halfway through the pastry. Then, spread all of your main filling onto the stack. Resume layering the pastry and the liquid mix until the pastry is finished. Then, fold the sides of the bottom layer over. Make sure you pour the remaining mix on top to prevent burning in the oven.

Leave the casserole dish in the fridge for 2-3 hours, this way it will be more crispy and tasty. Pre-heat the oven to 175 C (350 F). Bake until golden brown, for approximately 20 minutes.

Serve Talaş Böreği while still hot with Ayran, Cherry Compote or watermelon.

TALAŞ BÖREĞI

1 Pkt Puff Pastry (Tender flake 397 g)

Filling:

200 gr beef or lamb cut in cubes (lamb tastes better)
1 tbsp butter
1 small onion, sliced
1/2 cup sweet peas, frozen
2 tbsp crushed tomato in can
1 cup hot water
Salt
Pepper

On top:

1 egg, lightly beaten

First sautee the beef or lamb with butter, add the onion and cook for another 3-4 minutes. Add the rest of the ingredients along with 1 cup of hot water. Cook over low heat until most of the water evaporates.

For the Puff Pastry, follow the instructions on the box. Each block of pastry rolls out into a 12-inch (30 cm) square. Cut each dough in half to get rectangles. Equally divide and place the filling on one side of the rectangle. Fold, press the ends with your finger to close. Brush them with the egg on top. Put parchment paper on the oven tray, then place the Borek on it.

Preheat the oven to 175 C (350 F). Bake for about 15-20 minutes, until golden brown.

Mahlep is obtained from the fruits of the Idris Tree. It is used in a variety of dishes including Kandil Simidi. It also keeps the food fresh and makes it brittle.

SESAME SEED RINGS

(Susamlı Simit)

250 ml salted butter (room temperature)
60 ml olive oil
4 tbsp plain yogurt
1 tsp baking powder
3 cups flour (use fine strainer)
1 egg yolk
1 egg white
1 pkg sesame seed
1 pkg mahlep

First, pre-heat the oven to 175 C (350 F). Put all the ingredients above except the sesame seed and the egg white in a large plastic bowl. Use your hand to mix them well. Grab some dough the size of a little ball and shape it like a ring, with the diameter being approximately 2 inches.

First dip (only one side) in the egg white then in the sesame seed. Place on a baking tray. Repeat for the remaining dough and then bake for 20 minutes. This recipe will make 36 pieces.

Best served with Turkish Tea or milk.

SOFT TURKISH BAGEL

(Açma)

7 gr instant yeast
1/2 cup lukewarm milk
1/4 cup lukewarm water
2 1/2 tbsp sugar
1/2 cup sunflower oil
2 cup flour
1/2 tsp salt

Glaze:

1 egg white, lightly beaten
Nigella seeds (black sesame seeds)

Acma is a lovely breakfast or supper treat with Turkish Tea.

Mix the yeast with warm water in a large bowl. Stir well so the yeast dissolves, then add the suger, milk and sunflower oil. Stir until the sugar dissolves. Add flour and salt slowly and knead. Place the dough in a large bowl, cover it with plastic wrap over the rim and let it rest for about 2 hours until the dough rises to double its size.

Take a small sized ball from the dough and make it longer by spinning it. Then close up the ends to make a ring shape. Brush egg whites and sprinkle Nigella seeds on top.

Preheat the oven to 400 F. Place parchment paper on an oven tray and arrange the Acma on it. Bake for 10 minutes, then turn the heat to down 375 F then bake 15 more minutes until the tops take a golden colour.

This recipe makes 8-9 Acma.

LEEK AND FETA CHEESE BOREK

(Pırasa ve Beyaz Peynirli Börek)

1/2 cup yogurt
3/4 cup sunflower oil
3 eggs
3 sticks of leek, ends cut off, washed and finely sliced
1 cup feta cheese, crumbled
2 cups flour, sifted
1 tsp baking powder
1/2 tsp cayenne pepper (optional)
1/2 tsp black pepper
1 tsp salt

Preheat the oven to 400 F. Whisk the yogurt, eggs and sunflower oil in a deep plastic bowl. Toss in leek and feta cheese. Add the flour, baking powder, cayenne pepper, black pepper and salt. Knead using your hands. Pour into an oven-safe pyrex dish. Bake until the top gets nice golden colour - it should take about 30-35 minutes. Cut in square pieces with a knife. Serve warm or at room temperature with tea or Ayran for breakfast or a snack.

8-10 servings.

CATAL
(Çatal)

Catal are great for breakfast or as a snack with afternoon tea.

200 gr (about 1 ministick + 5 tbsp) unsalted butter, room temperature
2 1/2 tbsp sugar
1/2 cup sunflower oil
1/2 cup yogurt
3 cup flour
1/2 tsp salt
1 tsp baking powder
1 tsp mahlep, optional

Glaze:

1 egg yolk
2 tbsp black sesame seeds

In a large plastic bowl mix the butter, sugar, yogurt and sunflower oil with your hands. Add the flour, baking powder, salt and mahlep slowly and knead. Divide the dough in about 12 pieces and give each piece a long, rope-y shape with your hands. Place on the counter. For each piece, squeeze the two ends together and give it a canoe shape as seen in the picture.

Put parchment paper on the oven tray. Arrange the Catal on it. First eggwash tops, then sprinkle some black sesame seeds all over.

Preheat the oven to 400 F and bake for about 30 minutes until they are golden in colour. Bake in two batches with two oven trays. Makes approximately 12 Catal.

GOZLEME
(Gözleme)

The name Gözleme originates from the word "eye" (in Turkish göz means eye). When you start to cook it, you will see some little brown round shaped spots on it, which gives Gözleme its name.

See TurkishCookbook.com for preparation pictures.

Dough:

1 cup flour
A little bit less than 1/2 cup spring water, room temperature
1/2 tsp salt

Filling:

1/2 cup feta cheese, crumbled
1/4 cup parsley, chopped

Glaze:

1 tbsp butter, melted

Place the flour and salt in a bowl. Slowly add water while kneading. Put the dough on the lightly floured counter and knead well for about 10 minutes until it becomes smooth. Cover the dough with a damp paper towel, let it stand for 15 minutes.

Cut the dough in 4 equal pieces with a knife. Roll out each piece about 25 cm in diameter with a roller. Spread the filling ingredients equally in the middle of the dough. First fold the opposite sides to cover the filling. Then fold the 3rd side and lastly the 4th side to cover up the filling.

Continued...

Heat up the Teflon pan just under medium heat. Cook one side of Gozleme until there are some "brown eyes" on it. Then turn it over and brush this side with butter. Also brush the other side after cooking. Serve Gozleme while it is still warm with Ayran.

You can also make Gozleme with beef, spinach, potato or eggplant filling.

2 servings.

BEEF FILLING

150 gr lean ground beef
1 small onion, chopped
Salt
Pepper

Cook all the ingredients and sprinkle some chopped parsley on top.

SPINACH FILLING

1/2 pkg (150 gr) frozen chopped spinach, defrosted
1 small onion, chopped
1 tbsp olive oil
1/4 cup feta cheese, crumbled
1 pinch crushed pepper
Salt
Pepper

Saute the onion with olive oil. Add all the ingredients except feta cheese, cook for about 4-5 minutes. Turn the heat off, add feta cheese and stir.

POTATO FILLING

1 yellow potato, boiled, peeled, mashed
1 small onion, chopped
1 1/2 tbsp olive oil or butter
1/4 cup feta cheese, crumbled
1 pinch crushed pepper
Salt
Pepper

Saute the onion with olive oil, then add rest of the ingredients.

ROASTED EGGPLANT FILLING

1 medium sized eggplant, roasted, peeled, drained
1/4 cup Kasar or Mozzarella cheese, grated
1 tbsp olive oil
1 pinch crushed pepper
Salt
Pepper

Mix all the ingredients.

TAHINI BREAD
(Tahinli Ekmek)

Dough:

7 gr instant yeast
2 tbsp sugar
1 cup milk, warm
3 tbsp unsalted butter, room temperature
3 cups flour

Filling:

1 cup tahini (sesame seed paste)
1 cup sugar

Tahini Bread is a traditional Turkish Pastry which you can find at every Patisserie in Turkiye. You can have this very tasty pastry with your afternoon tea or coffee.

See TurkishCookbook.com for preparation pictures.

Start by mixing the filling ingredients. In a large bowl, melt the yeast with sugar and milk. Add in the butter and flour slowly, knead well. Cut the dough in 5 equal pieces with a knife. Roll out each piece until they are thin and a round shape (doesn't have to be perfectly round).

Spread the filling with a spoon on the doughs equally. Roll them up and let them sit for 30 minutes at room temperature on the counter. Then hold with each hand the ends of the roll and swing them in circles to get it longer and thinner. Then wrap them up like a cinnamon roll.

Place parchment paper on an oven tray and arrange the doughs on it. Let them rest for 10 more minutes. Preheat the oven to 400 F and bake for about 30 minutes.

CORN BREAD
(Mısır Ekmeği)

1 cup yellow corn meal
1 cup all purpose flour
1 tsp baking powder
1/2 tsp salt
1 cup milk
1/2 cup yogurt, plain
1 tsp sugar
2 eggs
1/4 cup extra virgin olive oil
1 tsp lemon zest

Mix the corn meal, flour, baking powder and salt in a large bowl.

Whisk milk, yogurt, sugar, egg and olive oil in another bowl. Stir into the dry ingredients and whisk. Pour the batter into the oiled Loaf Cake Mold.

Preheat the oven to 400° F (200° C). Place the mold on the middle rack. Bake for about 45 minutes. Place the Cornbread on the wire rack so it cools.

TURKISH RUSTIC BREAD

(Köy Ekmeği)

Sourdough Starter:

1/4 + 1/4 + 1/4 cup all purpose flour
3 tbsp + 3 tbsp + 2 tbsp warm water

Dough:

7 gr or 8 gr (1 packet) instant yeast
1 tsp sugar
1/4 cup warm water

3 cups flour, sifted
1 tsp salt
1 cup warm water

Getting the starter going takes a few days. On the first day, mix ¼ cup flour with 3 tbsp warm water in a bowl very well and cover. Let it sit at room temperature.

On the second day, add 1/4 flour and 3 tbsp warm water, mix very well, cover. Let it sit at room temperature.

On the third day, add 1/4 cup flour and 2 tbsp warm water, mix well. Let it sit at room temperature.

The starter will be ready on the fourth day. In a small bowl, mix the yeast, sugar and 1/4 cup warm water. Stir well so the yeast dissolves. Let it rest for 10 minutes - it will become bubbly.

Sift the flour and salt in a large bowl. Add the bubbly yeast mixture, 1 cup warm water and the sourdough starter. Mix and put the dough on the lightly floured counter and knead well for about 10 minutes until it becomes smooth.

Place the dough on a floured tray, sprinkle some flour over it and cover with a clean kitchen cloth. Let it stand in a warm spot*. After 2 hours the dough will double in size.

Place the dough on the lightly floured counter. Press all over it with your hands to get rid of air bubbles. Knead for about 3 minutes and give it an oval shape. Sprinkle some flour all over, cover it with a clean kitchen cloth, and put aside for about 40-45 minutes until the dough doubles again in size.

If you have a pizza peel, sprinkle some cornmeal on it. If not, place parchment paper on an oven tray and sprinkle some cornmeal or some flour on it. Then gently arrange the loaf on it. With a razor or very sharp knife make a few 1 cm deep slashes on the dough for the steam to come out.

Preheat the oven to 425 F and put some hot water in an oven-safe bowl. Place it at the bottom of the oven. Place the tray on the middle rack. Bake for about 40 minutes. Place the Turkish Bread on the wire rack to cool it. Then slice and serve.

* I turn the oven 175 C for 5 minutes and then off. After 5 minutes it was warm enough to make the dough double in size so I placed the tray in the oven for 2 hours.

See TurkishCookbook.com for preparation pictures.

TURKISH RAMADAN PIDE
(Ramazan Pidesi)

7 gr instant yeast
1 tsp sugar
1 3/4 cup warm milk
4 cup flour
1 tsp salt
1 tbsp olive oil

Glaze:

1 egg yolk
2 tbsp milk

After baking traditional Turkish Pide, let it cool for 5 minutes, then place in a clean plastic bag. It will be more soft this way.

See TurkishCookbook.com for preparation pictures.

In a small bowl, mix the yeast, sugar and 1/4 cup warm milk. Stir well so the yeast dissolves. Cover it with a towel, let it rest 15 minutes.

In a large bowl, sift flour and salt. Add the bubbly yeast mixture and 1 1/2 cup warm milk. Mix and put the dough on the lightly floured counter and knead well for about 10 minutes until it becomes smooth (no more crumbles). Then spread 1 tsp of olive oil inside a clean bowl. Place the dough in it and spread another tsp of olive oil with your hands all over the dough. Then cover it with a clean, damp towel. Put aside for about 1 to 1 1/2 hours at room temperature until the dough rises to double its size.

Place the dough on the lightly floured counter. Press all over it with your hands to get rid of air bubbles. Cut the dough in 2 pieces with a knife. Knead and give a ball shape to each, cover with a damp towel, and put aside for about 15 minutes. Place parchment paper on two oven trays, then arrange the doughs on the trays. Then use your palm to flatten each ball into a flatter rounded shape.

Lightly beat the glaze ingredients in a small bowl. Dip your finger tips in it and press all over the dough. Sprinkle some black or regular sesame seeds all over and cover with a clean damp towel. Leave for about 35-40 minutes to rise at a warm place.

Preheat the oven to 450 F and put some water in an oven-safe bowl. Place it on the bottom of the oven. Place one of the trays on the middle rack. Bake for about 8 to 10 minutes until the colour becomes light golden. Place the pide on the clean towel to cool it down a bit. Then bake the second dough. Serve while still warm.

BREAD WITH BLACK OLIVES
(Zeytinli Ekmek)

Dough:

7 gr or 8 gr (1 packet) instant yeast
1 tsp sugar
1/4 cup lukewarm water

3 1/2 cups all purpose flour, unbleached
1/2 tsp salt
3/4 cup lukewarm water
1/2 cup lukewarm milk

Filling ingredients:

1/2 cup black Turkish olives*, seeds discarded, cut in halves
1/2 cup extra virgin olive oil
1 medium sized onion, thinly sliced
1 tbsp oregano
1 tbsp lemon zest
1 tsp crushed red pepper

Loaf Cake Mold

Serve with tomato, feta cheese, cucumber and Turkish Tea for breakfast or lunch or dinner. It also goes great with Seafood recipes.

Mix the yeast, sugar and 1/4 cup lukewarm water in a small bowl. Stir well so the yeast dissolves. Let it rest for 15 minutes - it will become bubbly.

Sift the flour and salt in a large bowl. Add the bubbly yeast mixture, lukewarm water and lukewarm milk. Mix and put the dough on the lightly floured counter and knead well for about 15 minutes until it becomes smooth. Put the dough into a container with a lid. Keep it in the fridge overnight.

The following morning, place all the filling ingredients in a large bowl with the dough. Start kneading, but don't worry; the dough will absorb all the oil and the olives, just keep kneading with both your hands. When done, place the dough into the Loaf Cake Mold and put in a warm spot for about an hour until the dough doubles in size. With a razor or very sharp knife make 1 cm long deep slashes on the dough for the steam to come out.

Preheat the oven to 420 F at least 20 minutes before you start baking. Place the mold on the middle rack. After 30 minutes turn the heat down to 400 F and spray cold water on the dough. Bake for a total of 40 minutes. Place the Bread with Black Olives on the wire rack so it cools. Then slice it up and serve.

*Don't use ready-to-use sliced black olives that come in a jar or can. The taste won't be the same. Turkish olives are generally a bit wrinkly. Hopefully you can find some or similar ones at Turkish or middle-eastern stores.

DESSERTS

Baklava is of Turkish origin and is the world's favourite Turkish Dessert. It's extremely delicious.

See TurkishCookbook.com for preparation pictures.

TURKISH BAKLAVA
(Baklava)

Syrup:

> 1 1/4 cup water
> 1 3/4 cup sugar
> 1 tbsp lemon juice

Baklava:

> 454 gr (1 lb) Phyllo Pastry (~20-22 sheets)
> 1 cup + 3 tbsp unsalted butter, melted
> 1 1/2 cup pistachios, grounded (use a mixer but do not grind finely),
> the measurement is after grinding
> 6 tbsp cream 35%
>
> 3L (13x9x2") Pyrex casserole dish

To prepare the Baklava syrup place the water and sugar in a medium sized pot. First bring to a boil and continue boiling for 5 minutes. Then simmer for 15 minutes and turn the heat off. Add lemon juice and place the syrup in another bowl so that it cools down quickly.

Place the block of Phyllo sheets on the counter. Cut the sheets in half (8x12 inches). Now there are two blocks of approximately 40 sheets. After cutting in half, the size of the sheets should the same as the size of the Pyrex dish. Keep the blocks separate as half the sheets will go below the Baklava filling, and the rest above.

Brush the inside of the pyrex dish with the butter. Then lay down 2 sheets. Spread more butter on top, and then place two more sheets on top and butter again. Continue until you finish the first block of the phyllo sheets. Then brush on the cream evenly on top. Spread the pistachios on the cream evenly. Then finish second block of the sheets the same way. Don't forget to brush the very top with butter.

Dip a big, sharp knife into hot water to cut the Baklava in rectangles. Cut 4 vertically and 6 horizontally to get 24 piece of Baklava. However, don't cut all the way down, only cut halfway until you reach the pistachio. This will ensure only the top parts will rise when you bake it.

Preheat the oven to 375 F. Place the pyrex dish on the middle rack. Bake for 25 minutes. At this point turn the heat down to 325 F while the dish is still in the oven. Bake for 30 more minutes and take the Baklava out. Leave it at room temperature for 10 minutes.

Then using the same knife, re-cut the Baklava all the way down. This part may be a little bit hard but is worth it. With a tablespoon pour the lukewarm syrup evenly along the cut lines. Make sure not to pour it all over, only between the lines, otherwise Baklava won't turn out well. Sprinkle some pistachios on top of each Baklava. Let it rest at least 4 hours before serving. The syrup should be completely absorbed. You don't need to refrigerate it. Cover Baklava loosely with aluminum foil.

REVANI

Dry ingredients:

1/2 cup semolina
2/3 cup flour
1 tbsp baking powder

Wet ingredients:

1/2 cup granulated sugar
1 tbsp extra virgin olive oil
1 tsp vanilla extract
4 eggs

Syrup:

1 cup + 2 tbsp granulated sugar
500 ml water
4-5 drops lemon juice
8x8x2in oven Pyrex dish or regular cake tray

Serve Revani with Turkish Kaymak or thick cream and pistachios. Keep this dessert in the fridge.

Boil the syrup ingredients for a few minutes, put aside and let warm.

Use a mixer to blend the wet ingredients for a few minutes until the sugar melts. Then mix together the dry ingredients with a spoon in another bowl. Combine the two thoroughly, again using the mixer.

Butter the bottom and sides of the Pyrex and place in the mixture. Preheat the oven to 175 C (375 F) and bake for 25 minutes. Cut Revani into nine equal square pieces. Then pour the warm syrup on top while the cake is still warm. Use a tablespoon to do this and make sure to do it slowly so the cake absorbs the syrup equally. Let it cool.

SEMOLINA DESSERT
(İrmik Helvası)

1 cup semolina flour
125 ml unsalted butter
2 tbsp pine nuts

Syrup:

1 cup sugar
1 cup water
1 cup milk

You can put some chocolate sauce on top, if you like.

Cook the main ingredients on medium-low heat until golden brown in a large pot, constantly stirring. In another pot, mix the syrup ingredients until boiled. Pour the syrup very slowly into the pot with the semolina while stirring with a long wooden spoon. The mixture will be bubbly and will spit so be careful. Stir until the mixture leaves sides of the pot (it will become doughy), this shouldn't take more than a couple minutes.

Then place away from heat with the lid on, wait for 5 minutes and put in a bowl, levelled. When cooled, put it on a flat plate upside down. Serve in slices.

SULTAN'S JELLO

(Elmasiye)

> 3 cups orange juice, no pulp
> 1 cup water
> 1/3 cup corn starch
> 1/2 cup sugar
> 2 tbsp sesame, roasted

Melt the corn starch in 1 cup of water. Then add the sugar and orange juice, and put in a medium-sized pot. Cook on medium heat, stirring constantly. When you see bubbles on the surface, cook for one more minute. Then pour into small cups. Let them cool. Sprinkle the roasted sesame on top. Put them in the fridge and serve when cold.

If the orange juice is sweet, you don't need as much sugar. If you use orange juice sold in stores, don't add sugar.

NOAH'S PUDDING

(Aşure)

> 1 cup barley
> 1 cup white kidney beans (in a can), washed and drained
> 1 cup chickpeas (in a can), washed and drained
> 1 cup sugar
> 1 pkg vanilla or 1 tsp vanilla extract
> 10 cups water
> 10 dry apricots, soaked in water overnight, cut in pieces
> 10 dry figs, cut in pieces
> 1/2 cup raisins

Garnish:

> 1/4 cup walnuts, crumbled

Put 4 cups of water in a large pot along with the barley. Get it to boil on high heat. Then as soon as it boils, turn it down to medium-low heat and cook for about half an hour. Add the beans, chickpeas, vanilla, apricots, raisins, figs, sugar and 6 cups of hot water. Cook for about 45 minutes on medium-low heat. Stir occasionally. Pour into a large service bowl and let cool.

Keep Noah's Pudding refrigerated. When serving, garnish with crumbled walnuts. This recipe is one of the oldest and best known desserts of Turkish Cuisine. It's original name is "Aşure". When we cook Aşure, it is traditional to give some away to friends and family.

5000 years ago in Mesopotamia, Noah was King of the city Shuruppak. His was a trade empire, and he built a large trading ship. At that time, there was a raging flood and rainstorm. He and his family loaded animals, grain, fruit and beer onboard. The rain continued for 40 days. Afterwards there was no land in sight for 7 days. They ran out of drinking water and since the sea was salty, they had to resort to drinking beer. They eventually landed on Mount Ararat. The old saying goes that Noah's food was about to run out. He mixed and cooked all that he had left. The result became known as "Noah's Pudding".

APRICOT DESSERT
(Kayısı Tatlısı)

250 gr dry apricots
2 cups water

Syrup:

1 cup sugar
1 cup water

Garnish:

Turkish Kaymak or English devon cream or very thick cream
100 gr bleached almond
1/4 cup pistachio nuts, crushed

Soak the apricots in water overnight. Next day boil the syrup, drain the apricots and add into the syrup. Boil for 15 minutes and then let cool. To serve, spread half a teaspoon of cream and place an almond in each apricot. Garnish with pistachio nuts.

DRIED FIGS WITH WALNUTS
(İncir Tatlısı)

250 gr dried figs
1/2 cup sugar

Garnish:

1/4 cup walnuts, crumbled

Put the figs in a pot and cover them with water. Boil for about 20 minutes until they are softened over medium heat.

Drain and cut off the stalks. Place them in a medium pot and put the sugar on top. Add 2/3 cup water and cook about 25 minutes on medium-low heat. If necessary add more water. Leave some juice in it at about the same height as the top of the figs. Place on a service plate. Let cool, then garnish with walnut crumbs.

I suggest you use figs from Turkey as they taste better.

STRAWBERRY TOPPING
(Çilek Sos)

500 gr strawberries, washed, cut in 3 or 4
1/4 cup sugar

Place strawberries in a pot and pour the sugar on top. Heat it up for a minute, then turn the heat down to medium-low. Cook for about 20 minutes. Let it cool. Put into a jar with the lid closed and keep it in the fridge. Sprinkle sliced almonds on ice cream with the Strawberry Topping.

Mastic is used in preparation of Turkish ice cream and Turkish Delight. It is also used for pastry making, drinks, baked goods and chewing gum.

MASTIC PUDDING
(Sakızlı Muhallebi)

>4 + 1 cup milk
>1/2 cup cream, 35% (heavy cream)
>3/4 cup sugar
>1 tsp mastic, roll glass on the mastic to make it powdery (or use mortar)
>3 tbsp rice flour
>4 tbsp corn starch

Place 4 cups of milk, cream and sugar in a medium sized cooking pot. Melt the sugar over medium heat. Dissolve the corn starch and rice flour in 1 cup of milk and add into the pot. Then add the powdered mastic in it. Stir constantly for about 10 minutes to get it thick. Immediately pour into individual bowls. Let it cool down and sprinkle some pistachio on top. Keep it in the fridge before serving.

6 servings.

This dessert also goes well with ice cream.

CREAMY PUDDING
(Yalancı Tavukgöğsü)

>5 cups milk
>1 cup all-purpose flour
>1 cup sugar
>1 tsp vanilla extract
>1 tsp unsalted butter

Place all the ingredients except butter in a large pot. Stir constantly over medium heat. Add the butter when you see the bubbles on the surface. Boil one more minute while stirring. Take it off the stove. Pour into the blender. Blend for about 15 minutes over medium speed. Then pour the mixture into 2 a Lt Pyrex dish.

Let it cool for an hour. Cover the top and place in the fridge. If you like you can sprinkle some pistachios, coconut flakes or cinnamon on top before serving.

ALMOND PUDDING

(Keşkül)

4 cups milk
4 egg yolks
1 tsp almond extract
2 tbsp (30 gr) corn starch (melted with 3 tbsp water in a small cup)
1 cup sugar
1/2 cup almonds, bleached and ground

Beat the egg yolks, then whisk them with the sugar, almond extract, corn starch and milk in a bowl. Pour in a medium sized pot. Stir constantly on medium heat. Throw in the almonds when you see the bubbles on the surface. Boil one more minute while stirring. Take it off the stove. Pour into small serving bowls. Let them cool for an hour. Sprinkle some ground pistachio and/or shredded coconut on top. Chill them in the fridge with the tops covered.

6 servings.

You can serve Keskul cold by itself or with ice cream on top.

CHOCOLATE PUDDING

(Krem Şokola)

4 cups milk
3/4 cup sugar
1 tbsp corn starch
3 tbsp rice flour
1/2 cup water
1/3 cup cocoa
For each bowl: 2 tea biscuits, broken in half

Put 2 biscuits at the bottom of each bowl.

Melt the rice flour and corn starch with the water in a pot. Add sugar, cocoa and milk, and stir constantly on medium-high heat. When you see the bubbles on the surface cook for one more minute. Don't stop stirring. Pour in the bowls equally.

After letting them cool, place the bowls in the fridge. Serve cold and if you like, you can put vanilla ice cream on top.

6 or 7 servings.

SPINACH CAKE
(Ispanaklı Kek)

> 3 eggs
> 1 1/2 cup sugar
> 1 tsp vanilla extract
> ~500 gr spinach, roots cut off, washed, drained
> 1/2 cup extra virgin olive oil
> 2 tbsp lemon juice
> 2 1/2 cups flour, sifted
> 1 tsp baking powder

For on top:
> 1 cup whipped cream

Puree the spinach in a food processor, put aside. Whisk the egg and sugar in the mixer or by hand. Add the olive oil, lemon juice and pureed spinach in it and mix. Then add flour and baking powder. Mix for a few minutes. Pour into the oiled Pyrex (3L).

Preheat the oven to 375 F. Check with a toothpick to see if it's done, bake until it comes out clean. It takes about 30 minutes.

Let it cool down, then take it out of the Pyrex. Cut off the sides about 1 inch wide, and mix these using a blender to get them in powder form, put aside. Place the cake on a service plate. Spread whipped cream on the top, then sift the powdered cake on top of the cream. Slice it up and serve.

You can also substitute cherries with strawberries or other types of fruit and matching jello flavours.

CHERRY JELLO DESSERT
(Jöleli Pasta)

> 1 box (170 gr) of cherry jello
> 1 pouch (15 mL) of unflavoured gelatin
> 3 cups water
> 10 cherries, fresh or in a jar
> 5 tbsp yogurt
> 10 tea biscuits
> Cake mold with a hole in the centre

First, place the cherries in the mold, equally spaced apart. Pour 3 cups of boiling water in a plastic bowl, and mix in the gelatin and jello. Take one cup of this mixture and slowly pour on top of the cherries in the mold. Leave in the freezer for 15 minutes.

Take another cup of the mixture and add the yogurt in a separate bowl. Use a mixer to blend and then pour into the mold. Leave in the freezer for 15 minutes again.

Add the tea biscuits to the remaining one cup of the jello/gelatin mixture and blend again with the mixer. Pour into the mold and leave in the freezer for 15 more minutes.

To separate the dessert from the mold after you take it out of the freezer, place the mold in boiling water in your sink for 15 seconds. Place upside down on a serving plate.

BLACK EYE COOKIES

(Karagöz)

Dough:

375 gr unsalted butter, room temperature
1 cup sugar
3 1/2 cup flour
1 tsp vanilla extract

Filling:

3-4 tbsp strawberry jam

Garnish:

2-3 tbsp icing powder sugar
Round cookie cutter, 7.5 cm diameter

Serve Karagöz with afternoon tea.

To make the dough, mix the sugar and butter in a bowl. Then add the vanilla extract and flour. Slowly knead them together. Make a ball and cover with plastic wrap. Leave in the fridge for 15-20 minutes.

Preheat the oven to 375 F (190 C). Sprinkle some flour on the counter. Make 0.5 cm thick dough with the roller. Cut the dough with the round cookie cutter (7.5 diameter) to make 14 round pieces of dough. Put parchment paper on the oven tray and place the cookies on it. Bake for about 10-12 minutes. Immediately make two little holes on half of the cookies, so 7 of them, as shown in the picture. I used an apple corer for the little holes. Let them cool.

Spread strawberry jam with a knife on half of the cookies without the holes (so the other 7). Then sprinkle some icing powder over the other 7 cookies with the little holes. Stack them on the cookies with the jam.

TURKISH SHORTBREAD

(Un Kurabiyesi)

250 ml unsalted butter, room temperature
1/2 cup powdered sugar
1 tsp vanilla
2 cups flour
1/2 tsp baking powder

Garnish:

1/2 cup powdered sugar

Cream the powdered sugar and vanilla with butter, then slowly add the flour and baking powder. Make sure everything's well mixed. Make chestnut sized balls with your hands. Put parchment paper on an oven tray and arrange them on it.

Preheat the oven to 375 F and bake for about 15 minutes. Immediately sprinkle some powdered sugar on top using a small strainer after you take them out of the oven.

Makes 18-20 pieces.

BREAKFAST & EGGS

This delicious jam belongs to the Eagean Region, like fig and mastic jam.

GRAPE JAM
(Üzüm Reçeli)

> 500 gr small, green seedless grapes, washed, drained, stems removed
> 1/2 of a red apple, peeled, thinly grated
> 1 3/4 cup sugar
> 1 cup water
> 1 tsp vanilla
> 2 tbsp pine nuts, lightly roasted
> 1/2 of lemon juice

Melt the sugar, vanilla and water in a medium sized pot. Add the grapes and apple, and cook for about 45-50 minutes. Put a drop of jam on a cold plate, if it is not runny and stays, then it's done. Add the lemon juice and pine nuts, stir. After 2 minutes turn the heat off. Place into a clean jar, wait until it cools down, then close the lid tightly. Store in a dark and cool place.

PORTAKAL REÇELI
(Portakal Reçeli)

> 4 oranges, with thick skin
> 5 cups granulated sugar
> 1 lemon juice

Grate the orange rinds with thin side of the grater and place in a large pot. Cover with water. Cook on medium heat until they are softened, for about 45 minutes. Drain and put aside. Place the sugar in a pot and melt it with a little bit of water. Cut the oranges in chunks and throw them over the melted sugar. Cook for another 45 minutes on medium heat. Afterwards, squeeze the lemon juice on top and let it cool down.

TAHINI & GRAPE MOLASSES
(Tahin Pekmez)

> 1 cup tahini (ground sesame seed paste)
> 1/2 cup grape molasses (thick grape juice syrup)

Place tahini in a deep bowl, then slowly add grape molasses and mix them well. This traditional Turkish dessert should be eaten with Turkish Bread for breakfast or dessert. We especially like to eat Tahin Pekmez on cold winter days, it gives energy and is very filling.

TURKISH SCRAMBLED EGGS

(Menemen)

*4 eggs
1 cubanelle pepper, chopped bite size
4-5 medium sized tomatoes, chopped bite size
1/2 tbsp extra virgin olive oil
1/4 cup feta cheese, crumbled
Salt
Pepper*

Place the olive oil and cubanelle peppers in a large pan. Cook for about 2 minutes on medium-high heat. Then add the tomatoes, salt and pepper. Cook for another 7-8 minutes, stirring occasionally. Mix the eggs in a bowl, and pour into the pan. Then add the feta cheese. Keep stirring periodically until the eggs are done.

EGGS ON YOGURT

(Çılbır)

*1 cup plain yogurt with crushed garlic (room temperature)
2 eggs
3 cups water
1 tbsp vinegar
1 tbsp salt*

Garnish:

*1 tbsp butter
1 tsp red or cayenne pepper*

Place the yogurt with garlic on a service plate. Boil the water with the salt and vinegar in a large pot. After bubbling, turn down the heat to medium-low. Crack the eggs into the water side by side. Cover the lid and let the eggs cook for 3 minutes. Take the eggs out with a perforated spoon. Place the eggs over the yogurt on the service plate. Melt the butter in a small skillet and add the red pepper. Pour over the eggs when you see it start bubbling.

CLASSIC TURKISH BREAKFAST

(Klasik Türk Kahvaltısı)

Breakfast is very important in Turkish cuisine and has a rich variety. It can include Turkish Tea, butter, cheese (Beyaz Peynir, Kaşar, Tulum etc..), blackor green olives, eggs (soft or hard-boiled), homemade jam, cubanelle peppers, red peppers, tomato, cucumber and Pide or Turkish Bread.

POTATOES WITH EGGS
(Patatesli Yumurta)

> *1 cup hash browns, frozen*
> *2 tbsp extra virgin olive oil*
> *1 medium onion, sliced*
> *1 garlic clove, sliced*
> *2 eggs, beaten*
> *Salt*
> *Pepper*
> *1/4 cup fresh parsley, chopped*
> *1 pinch crushed red pepper (optional)*

In a large pan saute the onion with olive oil. Add in the garlic and hash browns (don't defrost), salt and pepper. Cook for about 10 minutes over medium-low heat, stirring constantly. Pour the beaten eggs over the potatoes and lightly stir with a wooden spatula. When the eggs are cooked (don't over-cook) sprinkle parsley and crushed pepper on top. Serve immediately as breakfast or a light meal with Tomato Salad.

* Instead of hash browns, you can use 2 medium sized potatoes. Peel and cut them in cubes and fry in sunflower oil. Then put them on a paper towel to soak up extra oil. Add the fried potatoes and the beaten eggs into the pan at the same time for this dish.

You can also have Kaçamak with Grape Molasses as a sweet dish. Heat up some butter, pour it on top and then add grape molasses.

KAÇAMAK

> *1/2 cup yellow cornmeal*
> *2 cup water*
> *1 tbsp sunflower oil*
> *1/2 tsp salt*

Sauce:

> *4 tbsp butter*
> *4 tbsp crushed tomato in a can, or 2 tbsp tomato paste mixed with water*
> *Crumbled feta cheese*
> *Pinch of crushed red pepper, optional*

Boil the water, sunflower oil and salt in a pot. Slowly pour in the cornmeal. Stir, making sure there are no lumps. Cook for about 10-12 minutes on medium-low heat. The mixture should become doughy and leave the sides of the pot in the end.

Meanwhile, cook the butter and crushed tomato for a few minutes on low heat.

Place Kaçamak on a service plate. Pour the tomato souce all over. Sprinkle some crumbled feta cheese and serve while hot. It's a very delicius dish for breakfast. You can also serve Kaçamak just with the Feta cheese.

TURKISH COFFEE
(Türk Kahvesi)

1 tsp Turkish Coffee
1/2 tsp sugar
1 Turkish Coffee cup of water, size pictured above
1 Turkish coffepot, called "cezve", as pictured above

Heat the stove on high heat. Put the sugar into the coffepot first, then add the coffee. Fill the Turkish Coffee cup with water at room temperature, although leave a bit of room at the top. Pour into the coffepot.

Place the coffeepot on the stove and slowly stir with a small spoon to ensure the coffee mixes in with the water. Then stop and wait until bubbles form at the top. When the bubbles rise, take the coffeepot off the stove and pour into the cup & serve.

The grinds will sink to the bottom of your cup, don't drink this part. The grinds are darker and thicker.

TURKISH TEA
(Türk Çayı)

4 tsp Turkish tea leaves + 2 tbsp bottled water
3 cups bottled cold water

Brewing Tea Turkish-style

To make Turkish tea you should use Çaydanlik which is a small tea pot-brewer (demlik) on top of a kettle.

Pour 3 cups of water into the larger kettle. Put the Turkish tea leaves and 2 tbsp of water into the teapot and place it on the kettle. Bring the water in the kettle to boil over medium heat. Then turn the heat off. Wait for the water to settle*, then pour half of the boiling water from the kettle over the leaves into the brewer. Let it brew for about 5 minutes**. Then pour the brewed tea into tea glasses using a small tea strainer. Fill in half of the tea glasses with the brewed tea and the rest with the hot water.

Serve Turkish tea with sugar cubes. I like to have my Turkish tea without sugar with just a few drops of lemon juice.

* If you pour boiled water immediately over tea leaves, the tea will lose its vitamins.

** If you extend brewing time, the taste will get bitter. Also freshly brewed Turkish tea should be consumed within half an hour of brewing time.

This recipe produces 4 servings in Turkish tea glasses.

Benefits of Turkish Tea

1. *Vitamins C and E in tea boosts the immune system and wards against leukemia.*

2. *Caffeine in tea stimulates the nervous system, increases concentration, makes you feel relaxed and comfortable.*

3. *Lowers cholesterol levels.*

4. *Fluoride in the tea helps prevent tooth decay.*

5. *Cleans the liver, lowers blood pressure, stabilizes the kidneys and it's also good for atherosclerosis.*

AYRAN

1 1/2 cup plain yogurt
1 1/2 cup water
1 tsp salt

This is very straight-forward but tastes great: Put all of the above in a blender. Mix for about 35-40 seconds. Pour into glasses. Also after blending, at the top, you will see bubbles and that's the best part. The drink shouldn't be thick.

4 servings.

Compote is a traditional dish which is served in individual bowls with Pilaf on the side.

RAISIN COMPOTE
(Üzüm Hoşafı)

1/2 cup Sultana or Golden raisins, stems cut off
1 1/2 cup water
1/4 cup sugar
3 or 4 cloves

Soak the raisins in warm water for about an hour, then drain.

Bring the sugar and water to boil in a medium cooking pot. Turn the heat down to very medium-low and add the raisins and cloves in it. Cook for about 10-12 minutes. Pour into a bowl and let it cool. Then chill in the fridge.

3-4 servings.

TURKISH COFFEE WITH MILK
(Sütlü Türk Kahvesi)

Broil 100 ml of homogenized (whole) milk in a small pot to get a layer of skin on the surface. Grab it with a spoon, along with a few tablespoons of milk, and place in a small glass cup or mug. Then make plain Turkish Coffee for one person. Pour it in over the milk.

If you like to have some sugar with your morning coffee, the Turkish way to do it is: Before taking a sip, put one cube in your cheek and start drinking. The sugar will melt in your mouth. When it is gone, replace with the second cube.

2530896

Made in the USA